THE
MEATBALL
SHOP
COOKBOOK

DANIEL HOLZMAN

AND

MICHAEL CHERNOW

with Lauren Deen

PHOTOGRAPHY BY JOHN KERNICK

BALLANTINE BOOKS · NEW YORK

THE
MEATBALL
SHOP

COOKBOOK

Published in the United States by Ballantine Books, an imprint of
The Random House Publishing Group, a division of Random House, Inc.,
New York.

BALLANTINE and colophon are registered trademarks of Random House, Inc.

Props and food styling by Alison Attenbourgh

ISBN 978-0-440-42316-4
ebook ISBN 978-0-440-42318-8

Printed in China on acid-free paper

www.ballantinebooks.com

9 8 7 6 5 4 3 2 1

First Edition

Book design by Liz Cosgrove

To my mother, Sherry;
my father, John;
and my big brother, Eli.
—*Daniel*

To my father, Mark;
my mother, Toni;
my sister, Nicole;
and my wife, Donna.
—*Michael*

CONTENTS

INTRODUCTION

GETTING THERE

We had talked about opening a restaurant together ever since we had our very first jobs as delivery boys for the Candle Cafe, a vegan restaurant (yeah, you read that right—*vegan*) on Manhattan's Upper East Side. We were thirteen, best friends, and we had big plans. We wanted to open our own place, a restaurant where our friends could hang out—a place created for us, by us.

After high school we both continued to work in the restaurant business. Daniel found his home in the kitchen, taking a job at the legendary Le Bernardin, and eventually moved out west to work in kitchens in Las Vegas, San Francisco, and Los Angeles, while Michael stayed in New York, polishing his skills working in the front of the house at a series of popular bars and restaurants. Michael eventually joined Daniel out west for a short time, but his heart belonged to New York, and he returned and soon after met his wife, Donna. Daniel knew that if he and Michael wanted to realize their dream of opening a place together, it would have to be in their hometown of NYC, so he soon returned as well. New York was home and filled with a supportive network of friends.

While we didn't know what neighborhood we wanted to be in yet, or what type of food we would serve, here's what we did know: We wanted a place that felt as if it had always been there, a staple, an institution. A place with better food than what you'd make at home. A place that would be a great date spot, sort of our take on the 1950s' roller rink/burger joint. A place that was casual (nothing overly fancy, intimidating, or chef driven) but most important, that you would be drawn to and that had an innovative, reasonably priced menu—a place where you could afford to become a regular. A place that was relaxed, with good energy, where you could listen to some killer music, eat great food, and meet some interesting people while you dug into your plate. A place that was warm, welcoming, and satisfying as well, kinda as comforting and eagerly anticipated as a bowl of delicious meatballs.

Because for us it was all about the balls.

SO WHY MEATBALLS?

We've been asked this question a *thousand* times. It all started with a joke.

Michael was working at a popular East Village Italian restaurant. Daniel would stop by occasionally late at night after work to catch up and hang out. Now, keep in mind that Michael is a marathon runner and generally healthy dude, and his daily late-night meal was the restaurant's staple rigatoni ragù minus the rigatoni. What was left was a bowl of meatballs and sauce that he'd eat alongside an order of broccoli, beets, or spinach. Daniel would come in and taunt him, saying things like "Be a man; eat a bowl of pasta," but sure enough, the one time Daniel caved and ordered the rigatoni "Mikey C style," he was hooked.

But we still weren't ready to have our lives revolve around meatballs. Initially we had a different menu and restaurant concept in mind, and we spent months chasing spaces and locations, only to miss out on each lease. We came closest on a space that had a walk-up window, which we figured we could use for "to-go" food. We brainstormed and cased the Lower East Side neighborhood at all hours, figuring out just what we could serve out of the window. What do you serve the hordes of young and hungries late at night? Something hearty, superdelicious, yet still healthy. . . . Of course, it had been sitting in front of us every night—Mikey C–style meatballs! And then we lost the space.

At first we were crushed, and then we snapped out of it with a big lightbulb moment—we said enough already, let's do fast food for our generation and open up an actual meatball shop. After all, wasn't Daniel tired of cooking fancy food at fancy restaurants charging a fortune? Wasn't our shared mission to reinvent fast food and elevate it to casual dining? Couldn't a meatball do all that and more? So, in the end we decided that there was no reason meatballs shouldn't be celebrated with their very own shop.

The food theme was decided. Familiar, accessible, affordable. Now we had to fine-tune and finance that dream.

UP ON THE ROOF

Like most good things, realizing our dream didn't come easy. But we stuck to it. We committed ourselves to hard work and went about developing the meatball concept. We reconfigured the numbers and wrote up a business plan. We pounded the pavement looking for locations, and we hosted a series of Sunday-night test suppers on Michael and Donna's roof in Williamsburg, Brooklyn. That's where we hammered it all out—where we developed the food, began to build the team, and fine-tuned the menu and service.

We sat out under the stars at a long table laden with a dozen different meatballs and stick to your bones sides and created the mix-and-match idea that became our signature theme. Here Donna, fresh out of pastry school, became our first official pastry chef, and concocted our single, revolutionary yet simple dessert, the cookie ice-cream sandwich. We crafted just the right amount of cookie-crunch ratio to creamy ice cream and cooled off the heat of those steamy summer nights with Donna's chocolate walnut meringue ice-cream sandwiches. These dinners were the heart and soul of what was to become The Meatball Shop.

Throughout those dinners we continued to go back and forth, arguing over the virtues of sauces and ball pairings, sides and ball pairings and ultimately realizing there's no right or wrong way to eat these balls. We decided to throw out the rules and not tell people what to order. We wanted to allow our guests to be in charge, to be able to customize their own meals, kind of like a choose-your-own adventure. Today, that's what makes the Shop so special—how many other restaurants give you a marker and a laminated menu and tell you to mix and match? Sure, we're happy to make suggestions and we have our own faves, but at the Shop, you're the boss.

84 STANTON STREET
LOCATION, LOCATION, LOCATION

We were ready to go. We knew the Lower East Side was where we had to be—we loved the energy, creative spirit, and history of the neighborhood. Determined, we pushed on and found just the right spot. The design and functionality of the space were as important to us as the food. As we said, we wanted to create a comfortable, casual, been-there-forever vibe, but did not want to have it feel like Grandma's house or self-consciously retro.

Wood was one key element to creating that warm feel, and we literally built that warmth into the restaurant by finding the wood through a friend who told us about a tenement building that was being gutted right around the corner from the Shop. We rolled up to this hundred-year-old building in a big rental truck and sure enough, they were gutting the building and happily gave us access to as many twenty-foot floor joists as we could handle. We grabbed around forty joists and drove them out to Michael's Uncle Curtis's woodworking shop in Queens, where Curtis cleaned them up and milled them for us. From true New York City history, we now have awesome wooden tables and a pretty handsome bar that lends authenticity and personality to the space. Thanks, Uncle Curtis. That's the thing about this city—you never know what treasure is right around the corner.

So now that the thing we had imagined for ten-plus years started to become a reality, we knew we had to thoughtfully consider every other detail, including the design of the space. We tiled the bar in an homage to NYC subways, and carefully chose the lighting. Lighting is very important—we wanted an amber glow throughout, so we chose vintage fixtures, fitted with reproduction Edison bulbs because they look awesome and shed just the right flattering light we were looking for. Let's face it, too. Everyone looks better in softer lighting, and the room feels intimate rather than cramped, even when it's packed with people on a rockin' Friday night.

KEEP FINGERS OUT OF MEAT GRINDER USE WOODEN TAMPER

Mike's vision for a cozy family-style joint also dictated the decor: We covered the walls with vintage black-and-white photographs (Mike spent a lot of time sifting through antiques stores to find the perfectly mismatched frames you'd find in your great-aunt's house). And Uncle Curtis's big communal table running down the center of the Shop became an easy way to connect all the different types of people we envisioned eating there.

FEBRUARY 9, 2010
OPENING DAY

The funny thing about friendship is how hard, how exciting, how tricky, how simple, how argumentative, and how supportive each interaction between friends can be. Mix in a business venture as risky and complicated as a restaurant, and you could have a recipe for disaster. That's why we're pretty damn proud that we were able to realize our dream and still remain best friends.

When we look across the dining room and see the team we built working together, and then we see all the diverse guests—and we mean diverse: tables of fashionable twenty-somethings rubbing elbows with local firemen or sanitation workers who are ordering takeout, standing next to tables of suited Wall Street execs—that's when we really get the power of meatballs. They're the great equalizer—our restaurant is

the crossroads for one big, complicated, amazing city. Meatballs can do all that. They're the real deal. Down to earth, universally loved, they make people happy. In fact, there have been so many happy people that we opened two more NYC shops earlier this year in Williamsburg, Brooklyn, and the West Village, to spread the meatball love.

THE BOOK

Now we want to spread the gospel of the balls to anybody willing to read about them. We think food should be enjoyed and not taken too seriously, and we want to share all that we've learned and created. It's all here—in every recipe headnote, sidebar, tip, and story. And while our balls play a starring role, we don't forget everything that goes along with them—from sauces to sides to fresh green-market vegetable dishes to decadent ice-cream sandwiches. All of our secrets are revealed in the pages that follow, so you are in for an adventure. Now you can customize your meals and your menus just as you would at the Shop—there are no rules here. Mix and match your balls, sauces, and sides; the possibilities are endless. Feel free to experiment and come up with some of your own favorite balls, then drop by the Shop and bring us a taste!

IT'S ALL ABOUT THE BALLS

In the Shop we usually make our meatballs about 1½ inches in diameter, and we include four balls per serving. In the book we offer the same 1½-inch balls and a variety of "mini" ¾-inch balls that are a good choice for a tasty first bite to serve with drinks or as hors d'oeuvres. You can make your meatballs as big or as small as you want—(just be sure to check their internal temperature [165°F] with an instant-read thermometer—because there really is no wrong way to make a meatball as long as it is fully cooked). Meatballs are easy and they're stress free—this is not a time to sweat the small stuff. There are, however, a few things to keep in mind that will make serving, eating, and storing your balls even easier.

MAKE AHEAD

Any of the meatballs in this book can be made a day in advance and then baked up to twenty-four hours later. Or they can be baked right away and kept in the fridge for up to three days and reheated (see below). In fact, they hold best when baked and then reheated.

SAUCING

Figure on ¼ cup of sauce per ball. We like to heat the balls right in the sauce. If you're serving the balls with pasta, then add cooked pasta right into the pan to soak up the sauce and flavor.

STORING

Store fully cooked meatballs in the fridge in a resealable container, in sauce or by themselves. They will keep for up to three days. Meatballs can also be frozen for up to two months, with or without sauce. Make sure to place them in a resealable container with a tight-fitting lid.

REHEATING

Meatballs can be reheated, with or without sauce, in the microwave for 4 minutes (6 if they're frozen); in a 300° oven, covered, for 20 minutes; or cooked stovetop in a covered sauté pan, with 2 to 3 tablespoons of water, for 10 minutes over medium heat.

MARKET : ROMAINE
SALAD : KABOCHA SQUASH
PICKLED RED ONION
SCALLION : PUMPKIN SEED
SHERRY VINAIGRETTE
AILY
REENS : KALE WITH
SOFRITO
OASTED : CAULIFLOWER
EGGIE : HAZELNUTS
CAPER VINAIGRETTE
ISOTTO : SAFFRO
CHIVE
EMONADE : POMEGRA
OOKIE : OATMEAL
RAISIN
CE CREAM :

THE

MEATBALL

SHOP

COOKBOOK

CHAPTER

1

THE BALLS

"MEATBALLS ARE THE ULTIMATE CURE-ALL FOR ANYTHING
THAT AILS YOU—HANGOVER, BREAKUP, LACK OF SLEEP,
EVEN A CRYING BABY."

CLASSIC BEEF MEATBALLS

Here they are—the top sellers at The Shop and sure to be a big hit at home. Most traditional meatball recipes call for Parmesan or pecorino cheese. While we're big fans of these stronger cheeses, we prefer ricotta. It's our secret weapon. The mild and creamy consistency of this fresh cheese gives the meatballs a unique, light texture. Beef has a subtle flavor, and the ricotta is a great way to add fat and moisture to the recipe without the overpowering flavor of a sharper cheese. These are quick to prep, and baking rather than frying makes this a fast comfort food even during the busiest of weeks.

Makes about 2 dozen 1½-inch meatballs

2 TABLESPOONS OLIVE OIL

2 POUNDS 80% LEAN GROUND BEEF

I CUP RICOTTA CHEESE

2 LARGE EGGS

½ CUP BREAD CRUMBS

¼ CUP CHOPPED FRESH PARSLEY

I TABLESPOON CHOPPED FRESH OREGANO
OR I TEASPOON DRIED

2 TEASPOONS SALT

¼ TEASPOON CRUSHED RED PEPPER FLAKES

½ TEASPOON GROUND FENNEL

4 CUPS CLASSIC TOMATO SAUCE (PAGE 56)

✤ Preheat the oven to 450°F. Drizzle the olive oil into a 9 × 13-inch baking dish and use your hand to evenly coat the entire surface. Set aside.

✤ Combine the ground beef, ricotta, eggs, bread crumbs, parsley, oregano, salt, red pepper flakes, and fennel in a large mixing bowl and mix by hand until thoroughly incorporated.

✤ Roll the mixture into round, golf ball–size meatballs (about 1½ inches), making sure to pack the meat firmly. Place the balls in the prepared baking dish, being careful to line them up snugly and in even rows vertically and horizontally to form a grid. The meatballs should be touching one another.

✤ Roast for 20 minutes, or until the meatballs are firm and cooked through. A meat thermometer inserted into the center of a meatball should read 165°F.

✤ While the meatballs are roasting, heat the tomato sauce in a small saucepan over medium-high heat, stirring often.

✤ When the meatballs are firm and fully cooked, remove them from the oven and drain the excess grease from the pan. Pour the tomato sauce over them. Return the meatballs to the oven and continue roasting for another 15 minutes.

ROASTED VS. FRIED VS. BRAISED

IS THERE A BEST WAY TO COOK A MEATBALL?

There is a bit of a debate when it comes to the best way to cook a meatball. Some people fry them in a skillet, some braise them in sauce, and some roast them in the oven. To us, there's really no contest, because we actually don't think there's a "best" way to cook a meatball.

At the Shop we like to roast them, simply because this is the fastest, easiest, most consistent way to cook a high volume of balls with great results. The recipes in this book usually call for roasting, but we encourage you to try sautéing, frying, and of course braising. You'll notice the outside texture of the ball changes a bit depending on the method, and you can play around and decide what you like—a bit of

a golden crust when sautéed or fried, or a bit more meltingly tender when braised.

When roasting meatballs, keep in mind that it is especially important to pack the balls tightly in the baking dish if you are planning to braise them afterward. This will help ensure that they are well formed. Braising the balls in hot liquid over time can cause them to fall apart, and the last thing you want is a big pot of broken balls. Also remember that unless your braising liquid is really well seasoned, the cooking process will take some of the salt out of the balls, so make sure to keep all that good flavor in and compensate by upping the salt in the recipe a bit.

BOLOGNESE BALLS

Both classic and inventive, these balls were one of the first meatball "specials" we served at the Shop, and they remain incredibly popular. While traditional Bologna-style meatballs call for braising in tomatoes and heavy cream, our version uses ground beef, with the tomatoes and cream added to the actual meatball. This makes for one mean spaghetti and meatballs.

Makes about 2 dozen 1½-inch meatballs

2 TABLESPOONS OLIVE OIL

1¾ POUNDS 80% LEAN GROUND BEEF

½ POUND MORTADELLA, CUT INTO ¼-INCH CUBES

2 LARGE EGGS

1 CARROT, FINELY DICED

1 CELERY STALK, FINELY DICED

1 ONION, FINELY DICED

¼ CUP CHOPPED FRESH PARSLEY

¼ CUP HEAVY CREAM

¼ CUP CRUSHED CANNED TOMATOES

1 CUP BREAD CRUMBS

1 TABLESPOON CHOPPED FRESH OREGANO
OR 1 TEASPOON DRIED

2 TEASPOONS SALT

1 TEASPOON FRESHLY GROUND BLACK PEPPER

✦ Preheat the oven to 450°F. Drizzle the olive oil into a 9 × 13-inch baking dish and use your hand to evenly coat the entire surface. Set aside.

✦ Combine the ground beef, mortadella, eggs, carrots, celery, onions, parsley, cream, tomatoes, bread crumbs, oregano, salt, and pepper in a large mixing bowl and mix by hand until thoroughly incorporated.

✦ Roll the mixture into round, golf ball–size meatballs (about 1½ inches), making sure to pack the meat firmly. Place the balls in the prepared baking dish, being careful to line them up snugly and in even rows vertically and horizontally to form a grid. The meatballs should be touching one another.

✦ Roast for 20 minutes, or until the meatballs are firm and cooked through. A meat thermometer inserted into the center of a meatball should read 165°F.

✦ Allow the meatballs to cool for 5 minutes in the baking dish before serving.

QUICK TIP

People have lots of tricks for rolling meatballs, but we've found that one of the best shortcuts to help cut down on time is to use a ¼-cup (2-ounce) ice-cream scooper. Simply pull a rounded scoop from the bowl of thoroughly mixed meatball mixture and drop it into the prepared baking dish, lining 'em up, one by one, as directed.

JAMBALAYA BALLS

Not so big, not so easy, but delicious nonetheless! These mini balls deliver the spirit and soul of one of the greatest food cities in the world—New Orleans. Down there, they make jambalaya a hundred different ways, and after a trip to Jazz Fest, we decided to try our hands at a NOLA-inspired ball. The results of our improv definitely sing—with all the essential Creole notes that surround the pork, chicken, sausage, and shrimp. While these balls are great solo, they also pair well with Classic Tomato Sauce (page 56).

Makes about forty ¾-inch meatballs

2 TABLESPOONS OLIVE OIL

I POUND GROUND PORK

I POUND GROUND CHICKEN, PREFERABLY THIGH MEAT

½ POUND ANDOUILLE SAUSAGE, FINELY DICED

½ POUND SHRIMP, SHELLED, DEVEINED, AND FINELY DICED

3 CUPS COOKED LONG-GRAIN WHITE RICE

I SMALL RED ONION, FINELY DICED

I RED BELL PEPPER, HALVED, SEEDED, AND FINELY DICED

2 LARGE EGGS

½ CUP BREAD CRUMBS

2 TABLESPOONS TOMATO PASTE

I GARLIC CLOVE, MINCED

I TABLESPOON SWEET PAPRIKA

I TEASPOON CRUSHED RED PEPPER FLAKES

PINCH OF CAYENNE PEPPER

I TEASPOON SALT

✤ Preheat the oven to 450°F. Drizzle the olive oil into a 12 × 17-inch rimmed baking sheet and use your hand to evenly coat the entire surface. Set aside.

✤ Combine the ground pork, ground chicken, sausage, shrimp, rice, onions, bell peppers, eggs, bread crumbs, tomato paste, garlic, paprika, red pepper flakes, cayenne, and salt in a large mixing bowl and mix by hand until thoroughly incorporated.

✤ Roll the mixture into round, ¾-inch meatballs, making sure to pack the meat firmly. Place the balls in the prepared baking dish, being careful to line them up snugly and in even rows vertically and horizontally to form a grid. The meatballs should be touching one another.

✤ Roast for 14 minutes, or until the meatballs are firm and cooked through. A meat thermometer inserted into the center of a meatball should read 165°F.

✤ Allow the meatballs to cool for 5 minutes in the baking dish before serving.

MINI BUFFALO CHICKEN BALLS

These balls will definitely get any party started. Buffalo's finest bar food minus the bones makes it the perfect food to serve up for the big game, a surprising appetizer, or even passed as a fancy hors d'oeuvre. It's the best part of hot and spicy wings with none of the mess. If you like your balls extra spicy, you can always add an extra tablespoon or two of hot sauce to the recipe. Make one batch and you'll know why these are a staff fave and top seller at the Shop. Serve with Blue Cheese Dressing (page 70).

Makes about forty ¾-inch meatballs

2 TABLESPOONS VEGETABLE OIL

4 TABLESPOONS (½ STICK) UNSALTED BUTTER

⅓ CUP FRANK'S REDHOT SAUCE OR ANY OTHER
FAVORITE HOT SAUCE

I POUND GROUND CHICKEN, PREFERABLY
THIGH MEAT

I LARGE EGG

½ CELERY STALK, MINCED

¾ CUP BREAD CRUMBS

I TEASPOON SALT

✤ Preheat the oven to 450°F. Drizzle the vegetable oil into a 9 × 13-inch baking dish and use your hand to evenly coat the entire surface. Set aside.

✤ Combine the butter and hot sauce in a small saucepan, and cook over low heat, whisking until the butter is melted and fully incorporated. Remove from the heat and allow the mixture to cool for 10 minutes.

✤ Combine the hot sauce mixture, ground chicken, egg, celery, bread crumbs, and salt in a large mixing bowl and mix by hand until thoroughly incorporated.

✤ Roll the mixture into round, ¾-inch balls, making sure to pack the meat firmly. Place the balls in the prepared baking dish, being careful to line them up snugly and in even rows vertically and horizontally to form a grid. The meatballs should be touching one another.

✤ Roast for 15 to 20 minutes, or until the meatballs are firm and cooked through. A meat thermometer inserted into the center of a meatball should read 165°F.

✤ Allow the meatballs to cool for 5 minutes in the baking dish before serving.

When we think of sun-drenched Greece, we think of olives, feta cheese, preserved lemons, and oregano. These salty, tangy, and fragrant ingredients instantly transport us to the Mediterranean islands. These meatballs capture the essence of Greek flavors and roll it all up into a meatball. You can buy preserved lemons, but our quickie recipe below is a no-brainer. Serve with a big ladleful of Classic Tomato Sauce (page 56).

Makes about 2 dozen 1½-inch meatballs

2 TABLESPOONS OLIVE OIL

2 POUNDS GROUND LAMB

2 LARGE EGGS

½ CUP BREAD CRUMBS

¼ CUP PITTED, CHOPPED KALAMATA OLIVES

¼ CUP CHOPPED FRESH PARSLEY

3 TABLESPOONS CRUMBLED FETA CHEESE

3 TABLESPOONS CHOPPED FRESH MINT

I TABLESPOON CHOPPED FRESH OREGANO
OR I TEASPOON DRIED

I SMALL GARLIC CLOVE, MINCED

I½ TEASPOONS SALT

¼ QUICK PRESERVED LEMON, CHOPPED
(RECIPE FOLLOWS)

✤ Preheat the oven to 450°F. Drizzle the olive oil into a 9 × 13-inch baking dish and use your hand to evenly coat the entire surface. Set aside.

✤ Combine the ground lamb, eggs, bread crumbs, olives, parsley, feta, mint, oregano, garlic, salt, and preserved lemon in a large mixing bowl and mix by hand until thoroughly incorporated.

✤ Roll the mixture into round, golf ball–size meatballs (about 1½ inches), making sure to pack the meat firmly. Place the balls in the prepared baking dish, being careful to line them up snugly and in even rows vertically and horizontally to form a grid. The meatballs should be touching one another.

✤ Roast for 20 minutes, or until the meatballs are firm and cooked through. A meat thermometer inserted into the center of a meatball should read 165°F.

✤ Allow the meatballs to cool for 5 minutes in the baking dish before serving.

～ QUICK PRESERVED LEMON ～

Don't be surprised by the texture of these preserved lemons—the inside is very soft and the outside has a bit of firmness. Use the lemons in vinaigrettes, with white beans, as a rub for steak or roast chicken, or in a marinade or sauce for chicken or seafood. They'll keep for a week in the refrigerator.

I LEMON
½ CUP SALT

Bring 2 quarts water to a rolling boil in a saucepan over high heat. Add the lemon and salt and bring back to a boil for 15 minutes. Remove the lemon from the water and allow to cool.

BBQ PORK BALLS

When a prominent bourbon company called and asked if we would develop a meatball for them, we were all over it—we had wanted to run a BBQ meatball on the menu since the Shop opened. All that was needed was a Lower East Side (L.E.S.) barbecue sauce, which, when mixed with some sautéed onions and freshly ground pork, became the official recipe for the Shop's BBQ balls. So the next time you want some quick 'cue, instead of slaving over the grill, you can prepare these balls ahead and spend some QT with your guests.

Makes about 2 dozen 1½-inch meatballs

3 TABLESPOONS OLIVE OIL

I SMALL ONION, FINELY DICED

2 POUNDS GROUND PORK

I CUP L.E.S. BARBECUE SAUCE (PAGE 61)

2 LARGE EGGS

¾ CUP BREAD CRUMBS

I TEASPOON SALT

✤ Preheat the oven to 450°F. Drizzle 2 tablespoons of the olive oil into a 9 × 13-inch baking dish and use your hand to evenly coat the entire surface. Set aside.

✤ Heat the remaining 1 tablespoon olive oil in a medium frying pan over medium-high heat. Add the onions and cook, stirring frequently, until they are soft and well browned, 8 to 10 minutes. Transfer to a plate and let cool in the refrigerator.

✤ When the onions have cooled, combine them with the ground pork, barbecue sauce, eggs, bread crumbs, and salt in a large mixing bowl and mix by hand until thoroughly incorporated.

✤ Roll the mixture into round, golf ball–size meatballs (about 1½ inches), making sure to pack the meat firmly. Place the balls in the prepared baking dish, being careful to line them up snugly and in even rows vertically and horizontally to form a grid. The meatballs should be touching one another.

✤ Roast for 20 minutes, or until the meatballs are firm and cooked through. A meat thermometer inserted into the center of a meatball should read 165°F.

✤ Allow the meatballs to cool for 5 minutes in the baking dish before serving.

CHICKEN MEATBALLS

These are the sleeper hit at the Shop and star in our Chicken Parm slider. Guests are always surprised by the moistness and rich taste of these balls, and the secret is ground thigh meat. Chicken thighs are packed with flavor and are a better choice than the usual dry breast meat. Try these balls with Spinach-Basil Pesto (page 58) or Parmesan Cream Sauce (page 60). You can substitute ground turkey if you can't find ground chicken.

Makes about 2 dozen 1½-inch meatballs

2 TABLESPOONS OLIVE OIL

2 POUNDS GROUND CHICKEN, PREFERABLY THIGH MEAT

2 LARGE EGGS

½ CUP BREAD CRUMBS

½ CUP CHOPPED FRESH PARSLEY

¼ CUP DRY WHITE WINE

I TABLESPOON SALT

I TEASPOON GROUND FENNEL

I TEASPOON FRESHLY GROUND BLACK PEPPER

✤ Preheat the oven to 450°F. Drizzle the olive oil into a 9 × 13-inch baking dish and use your hand to evenly coat the entire surface. Set aside.

✤ Combine the ground chicken, eggs, bread crumbs, parsley, white wine, salt, fennel, and pepper in a large mixing bowl and mix by hand until thoroughly incorporated.

✤ Roll the mixture into round, golf ball–size meatballs (about 1½ inches), making sure to pack the meat firmly. Place the balls in the prepared baking dish, being careful to line them up snugly and in even rows vertically and horizontally to form a grid. The meatballs should be touching one another.

✤ Roast for 20 minutes, or until the meatballs are firm and cooked through. A meat thermometer inserted into the center of a meatball should read 165°F.

✤ Allow the meatballs to cool for 5 minutes in the baking dish before serving.

THE BALLS

THE SPANIARD

Here earthy ingredients from sunny Spain come together for a richly flavored meatball. A sharp Manchego sheep's milk cheese and paprika-spiced chorizo sausage are mixed with ground pork and just a hint of red pepper flakes and garlic. When rolled into minis, these are a tapas treat. These balls stand up to the Spicy Meat Sauce (page 57) but go just as well with Classic Tomato Sauce (page 56).

Makes about 2 dozen 1½-inch meatballs

2 TABLESPOONS OLIVE OIL

I POUND GROUND PORK

½ POUND DRY SPANISH CHORIZO, FINELY DICED

½ POUND MANCHEGO CHEESE, FINELY DICED

3 CUPS COOKED LONG-GRAIN WHITE RICE

2 LARGE EGGS

½ CUP BREAD CRUMBS

2 TABLESPOONS TOMATO PASTE

I GARLIC CLOVE, MINCED

I TEASPOON CRUSHED RED PEPPER FLAKES

I TEASPOON SALT

✛ Preheat the oven to 450°F. Drizzle the olive oil into a 9 × 13-inch baking dish and use your hand to evenly coat the entire surface. Set aside.

✛ Combine the ground pork, chorizo, Manchego, rice, eggs, bread crumbs, tomato paste, garlic, red pepper flakes, and salt in a large mixing bowl and mix by hand until thoroughly incorporated.

✛ Roll the mixture into round, golf ball–size meatballs (about 1½ inches), making sure to pack the meat firmly. Place the balls in the prepared baking dish, being careful to line them up snugly and in even rows vertically and horizontally to form a grid. The meatballs should be touching one another.

✛ Roast for 20 minutes, or until the meatballs are firm and cooked through. A meat thermometer inserted into the center of a meatball should read 165°F.

✛ Allow the meatballs to cool for 5 minutes in the baking dish before serving.

THE BALLS

FIGHTIN' IRISH BALLS

At the Shop we think all holidays deserve their own meatball. In New York City, Saint Patrick's Day is a big deal, celebrated with a major parade, and so of course a meatball was born. These are a clever twist on the usual corned beef and cabbage pairing, and they were so popular that now we serve them throughout the year. We're not fans of artificial coloring but we suppose you could even dye them green if you wanted to. We love to serve them with Mashed Potatoes (page 79) and Mushroom Gravy (page 63).

Makes about 2 dozen 1½-inch meatballs

2 TABLESPOONS OLIVE OIL

1½ POUNDS COOKED CORNED BEEF,
FINELY CHOPPED

½ POUND GROUND PORK

2 CUPS MASHED POTATOES (PAGE 79),
AT ROOM TEMPERATURE

I CUP FINELY DICED GREEN CABBAGE

2 LARGE EGGS

½ CUP BREAD CRUMBS

2 TABLESPOONS WHOLE GRAIN MUSTARD

I TEASPOON SALT

½ TEASPOON FRESHLY GROUND BLACK PEPPER

✤ Preheat the oven to 450°F. Drizzle the olive oil into a 9 × 13-inch baking dish and use your hand to evenly coat the entire surface. Set aside.

✤ Combine the corned beef, ground pork, potatoes, cabbage, eggs, bread crumbs, mustard, salt, and pepper in a large mixing bowl and mix by hand until thoroughly incorporated.

✤ Roll the mixture into round, golf ball–size meatballs (about 1½ inches), making sure to pack the meat firmly. Place the balls in the prepared baking dish, being careful to line them up snugly and in even rows vertically and horizontally to form a grid. The meatballs should be touching one another.

✤ Roast for 20 minutes, or until the meatballs are firm and cooked through. A meat thermometer inserted into the center of a meatball should read 165°F.

✤ Allow the meatballs to cool for 5 minutes in the baking dish before serving.

THE BALLS

VEGGIE BALLS

Sometimes you just gotta take a break from hard-core carnivordom, and these are the way to go—just ask our staff, who eat them around the clock. These balls happen to be Mike's favorite, too. You'll often find us at the bar with a big bowl, topped with Classic Tomato Sauce (page 56) or Spinach-Basil Pesto (page 58) and a side of steamed or sautéed spinach. And when it comes to kids, this is a great and tasty way to sneak in more veggies.

Makes about 2 dozen 1½-inch meatballs

2 CUPS LENTILS

¼ CUP PLUS 2 TABLESPOONS OLIVE OIL

I LARGE ONION, CHOPPED

2 CARROTS, CHOPPED

2 CELERY STALKS, CHOPPED

I GARLIC CLOVE, MINCED

I TABLESPOON CHOPPED FRESH THYME

2 TEASPOONS SALT

3 TABLESPOONS TOMATO PASTE

8 OUNCES BUTTON MUSHROOMS,
WIPED CLEAN AND SLICED

3 LARGE EGGS

½ CUP GRATED PARMESAN CHEESE

½ CUP BREAD CRUMBS

½ CUP CHOPPED FRESH PARSLEY

¼ CUP FINELY CHOPPED WALNUTS

✤ Combine the lentils and 2 quarts water in a medium stockpot and bring to a boil over high heat. Reduce the heat to low and simmer until the lentils are soft (but not falling apart), about 25 minutes. Drain the lentils and allow to cool.

✤ Add ¼ cup of the olive oil to a large frying pan and sauté the onions, carrots, celery, garlic, thyme, and salt over medium-high heat, stirring frequently, for about 10 minutes, until the vegetables are tender and just beginning to brown. Add the tomato paste and continue to cook, stirring constantly, for 3 minutes. Add the mushrooms and cook, stirring frequently, for 15 more minutes, or until all the liquid is absorbed. Transfer the mixture to a large bowl and allow to cool to room temperature. When cool, add the lentils to the vegetable mixture.

✤ Add the eggs, Parmesan, bread crumbs, parsley, and walnuts to the cooled vegetable mixture and mix by hand until thoroughly incorporated. Place in the refrigerator for 25 minutes.

✤ Preheat the oven to 400°F.

✤ Drizzle the remaining 2 tablespoons olive oil into a 9 × 13-inch baking dish and use your hand to evenly coat the entire surface. Set aside.

(Continued on page 18)

✦ Roll the mixture into round, golf ball–size meatballs (about 1½ inches), making sure to pack the vegetable mixture firmly. Place the balls in the prepared baking dish, allowing ¼-inch of space between the balls and place them in even rows vertically and horizontally to form a grid.

✦ Roast for 30 minutes, or until the meatballs are firm and cooked through.

✦ Allow the meatballs to cool for 5 minutes in the baking dish before serving.

MINI CRAB CAKE BALLS

Call them meatballs or call them crab cakes. Either way, they're an addictive hit. The succulent sweetness of crab is paired with classic Old Bay Seasoning, but it gets a texture twist with the addition of crunchy, salty potato chips. This is the perfect party snack or starter, and it can be thrown together and ready in under fifteen minutes. Serve these balls skewered with toothpicks, with our Classic Tomato Sauce (page 56) or with tartar sauce, or toss them with pasta and tomato sauce for a hearty seafood pasta.

Makes about thirty ¾-inch meatballs

2 TABLESPOONS OLIVE OIL

I POUND JUMBO LUMP CRABMEAT,
PICKED OVER FOR SHELLS

1½ CUPS CRUSHED KETTLE-COOKED
POTATO CHIPS

½ CUP MAYONNAISE

I LARGE EGG

¼ CUP BREAD CRUMBS

2 TABLESPOONS OLD BAY SEASONING

½ TEASPOON SALT

JUICE FROM ½ LEMON

✤ Preheat the oven to 450°F. Drizzle the olive oil into a 9 × 13-inch baking dish and use your hand to evenly coat the entire surface. Set aside.

✤ Combine the crabmeat, potato chips, mayonnaise, egg, bread crumbs, Old Bay seasoning, salt, and lemon juice in a large mixing bowl and mix by hand until thoroughly incorporated.

✤ Roll the mixture into round ¾-inch balls, making sure to pack the mixture firmly. Place the balls in the prepared baking dish, being careful to line them up snugly and in even rows vertically and horizontally to form a grid. The balls should be touching one another.

✤ Roast for 10 minutes, or until the meatballs are firm and cooked through.

✤ Allow the meatballs to cool for 5 minutes in the baking dish before serving.

SPICY PORK MEATBALLS

With just enough spice to tickle the tongue, these balls are the ultimate crowd-pleasers. Whenever we have a large event to cook for, we always bring our Spicy Pork Balls. In terms of the meat for these balls, ask your butcher to grind some pork shoulder. It's inexpensive and full of flavor, and it's a cut we really love. Instead of using bread crumbs, as we do with most meatballs, we use fresh white bread, which makes for a lighter meatball. The ideal way to serve these is over a bed of Creamy Polenta (page 78) with a hearty ladleful of Spicy Meat Sauce (page 57).

Makes about 2 dozen 1½-inch meatballs

2 TABLESPOONS OLIVE OIL

2 POUNDS PORK SHOULDER, GROUND

I TABLESPOON PLUS I TEASPOON SALT

4 JARRED HOT CHERRY PEPPERS, MINCED

¼ CUP HOT CHERRY PEPPER PICKLING LIQUID

4 SLICES FRESH WHITE BREAD, MINCED

3 LARGE EGGS

✤ Preheat the oven to 450°F. Drizzle the olive oil into a 9 × 13-inch baking dish and use your hand to evenly coat the entire surface. Set aside.

✤ Combine the ground pork, salt, cherry peppers, pickling liquid, bread, and eggs in a large mixing bowl and mix by hand until thoroughly incorporated.

✤ Roll the mixture into round, golf ball–size meatballs (about 1½ inches), making sure to pack the meat firmly. Place the balls in the prepared baking dish, being careful to line them up snugly and in even rows vertically and horizontally to form a grid. The meatballs should be touching one another.

✤ Roast for 20 minutes, or until the meatballs are firm and cooked through. A meat thermometer inserted into the center of a meatball should read 165°F.

✤ Allow the meatballs to cool for 5 minutes in the baking dish before serving.

BOUILLABAISSE BALLS

The aromatic flavors of a rich fish stew all rolled up in a ball—how'd we do it? A generous splash of Pernod, along with a pinch of fragrant saffron, transports you straight to the Mediterranean coast. We use a firm white fish like tilapia, but feel free to substitute any similarly textured fish. Serve these alongside any of the risottos offered in Chapter 3 (see pages 74 to 77).

Makes about 2 dozen 1½-inch meatballs

4 TABLESPOONS OLIVE OIL

I ONION, FINELY DICED

2 CELERY STALKS, FINELY DICED

2 GARLIC CLOVES, MINCED

¼ TEASPOON CRUSHED RED PEPPER FLAKES

PINCH OF CAYENNE PEPPER (OPTIONAL)

PINCH OF SAFFRON THREADS

2 TEASPOONS SALT

¼ CUP TOMATO PASTE

2 TABLESPOONS PERNOD

2 POUNDS WHITE FISH, SUCH AS TILAPIA OR PERCH, GROUND OR FINELY CHOPPED

½ CUP CHOPPED FRESH PARSLEY

2 LARGE EGGS

I CUP BREAD CRUMBS

✦ Preheat the oven to 450°F. Drizzle 2 tablespoons of the olive oil into a 9 × 13-inch baking dish and use your hand to evenly coat the entire surface. Set aside.

✦ Heat the remaining 2 tablespoons olive oil in a medium frying pan over medium-high heat. Add the onions, celery, garlic, red pepper flakes, cayenne (if using), saffron, and salt and cook, stirring frequently, until the vegetables are soft and translucent, about 10 minutes. Add the tomato paste, lower the heat to medium, and continue to cook, stirring constantly, for 5 minutes, taking care that the paste does not burn and cooks evenly. Add the Pernod, stir to incorporate, and transfer the mixture to a bowl. Place in the refrigerator to cool.

✦ When the vegetables have cooled completely, combine them with the fish, parsley, eggs, and bread crumbs in a large mixing bowl and mix by hand until thoroughly incorporated.

✦ Roll the mixture into round, golf ball–size meatballs (about 1½ inches), making sure to pack the meat firmly. Place the balls in the prepared baking dish, being careful to line them up snugly and in even rows vertically and horizontally to form a grid. The meatballs should be touching one another.

✦ Roast for 20 minutes, or until the meatballs are firm and cooked through. A meat thermometer inserted into the center of a meatball should read 155°F.

✦ Allow the meatballs to cool for 5 minutes in the baking dish before serving.

MEDITERRANEAN LAMB BALLS

When we opened the Shop, these Mediterranean balls were our first daily special. We were so busy that we didn't get a chance to change it for three weeks, but nobody really complained because they were so delicious. People still get excited when we bring them back for a day or two. The raisins and walnuts give this ball a subtly sweet and earthy quality that complements the lamb. Make these into mini balls and pass them around at your next party. Just add toothpicks and Spanish-Basil Pesto (page 58) for dip. No sauce required. Or serve them over a bed of Braised Kale with Anchovies and Garlic (page 93) or Creamed Spinach (page 100).

Makes about 2 dozen 1½-inch balls

2 TABLESPOONS OLIVE OIL

2 POUNDS GROUND LAMB

3 LARGE EGGS

I CUP DARK RAISINS, CHOPPED

½ CUP WALNUT HALVES, FINELY CHOPPED

½ CUP CHOPPED FRESH PARSLEY

½ CUP CHOPPED FRESH MINT

½ CUP BREAD CRUMBS

2 TEASPOONS SALT

I TEASPOON FRESHLY GROUND BLACK PEPPER

❖ Preheat the oven to 450°F. Drizzle the olive oil into a 9 × 13-inch baking dish and use your hand to evenly coat the entire surface. Set aside.

❖ Combine the ground lamb, eggs, raisins, walnuts, parsley, mint, bread crumbs, salt, and pepper in a large mixing bowl and mix by hand until thoroughly incorporated.

❖ Roll the mixture into round, golf ball–size meatballs (about 1½ inches), making sure to pack the meat firmly. Place the balls in the prepared baking dish, being careful to line them up snugly and in even rows vertically and horizontally to form a grid. The meatballs should be touching one another.

❖ Roast for 20 minutes, or until the meatballs are firm and cooked through. A meat thermometer inserted into the center of a meatball should read 165°F.

❖ Allow the meatballs to cool for 5 minutes in the baking dish before serving.

Bread crumbs are an important supporting cast member in our ballapalooza. They lighten the density of the meat and provide a great canvas for the seasonings. We have some preferences for which ones work best.

While flavored bread crumbs might make for a mean chicken cutlet, meatballs call for something with a more neutral flavor. Any store-bought plain bread crumbs should work well with meatballs (although we suggest you avoid panko [Japanese-style] bread crumbs, as their texture is a bit too rough).

If you are feeling adventurous or have some extra time (and bread) on your hands, try making your own bread crumbs. At the Shop we are lucky enough to have Ramon Eduardo from Il Forno bakery bake our bread, and we hate to waste such well-crafted loaves, so we save all of our old bread for crumbs for the next day's balls.

Start with some day-old crusty white bread. (You want to avoid anything with cinnamon, fruit, or whole nuts in it). Allow the bread to dry out completely, usually a day or two, depending on humidity and the size of the bread pieces (if you are short on time, try drying the bread in a warm 200°F oven for 20 minutes or so). Once the bread is completely dry and crispy, break it up and pulse in a food processor until it resembles the consistency of sand. Strain through a mesh sieve. Process any larger chunks of bread that don't fit through the sieve, then sieve again.

The bread crumbs can be used immediately or stored in a container with a tight-fitting lid for up to 2 months in the pantry or up to 6 months in the freezer.

VIVA LA MÉXICO BALLS

The vibrant flavors of Mexico pop in these balls that we created for a Cinco de Mayo party. Pork meatballs get a kick from a splash of tequila, the smoky heat of ancho and guajillo chiles, along with a fragrant touch of cinnamon and cumin, reminiscent of carnitas, the traditional Mexican spiced, braised pork. Serve these with Salsa Roja (page 66). To serve alongside margaritas, try them as mini balls.

Makes 2 dozen 1½-inch meatballs

2 TABLESPOONS OLIVE OIL

1 DRIED ANCHO CHILE, STEMMED, SEEDED, AND MINCED

1 DRIED GUAJILLO CHILE, STEMMED, SEEDED, AND MINCED

¼ CUP TEQUILA

JUICE FROM 1 LIME

2 POUNDS GROUND PORK

1½ CUPS COOKED LONG-GRAIN WHITE RICE

2 LARGE EGGS

½ CUP BREAD CRUMBS

3 SOFT CORN TORTILLAS, MINCED

1 SMALL ONION, FINELY DICED

½ BUNCH FRESH CILANTRO, CHOPPED (INCLUDING STEMS)

2 TABLESPOONS TOMATO PASTE

1 GARLIC CLOVE, MINCED

1 TEASPOON CRUSHED RED PEPPER FLAKES

1 TEASPOON SALT

½ TEASPOON GROUND CUMIN

PINCH OF GROUND CINNAMON

✤ Preheat the oven to 450°F. Drizzle the olive oil into a 9 × 13-inch baking dish and use your hand to evenly coat the entire surface. Set aside.

✤ Combine the ancho chile, guajillo chile, tequila, and lime juice in a small bowl and let sit for 5 minutes.

✤ Combine the chile mixture with the ground pork, rice, eggs, bread crumbs, tortillas, onions, cilantro, tomato paste, garlic, red pepper flakes, salt, cumin, and cinnamon in a large mixing bowl and mix by hand until thoroughly incorporated.

✤ Roll the mixture into round, golf ball–size meatballs (about 1½ inches), making sure to pack the meat firmly. Place the balls in the prepared baking dish, being careful to line them up snugly and in even rows vertically and horizontally to form a grid. The meatballs should be touching one another.

✤ Roast for 20 minutes, or until the meatballs are firm and cooked through. A meat thermometer inserted into the center of a meatball should read 165°F.

✤ Allow the meatballs to cool for 5 minutes in the baking dish before serving.

GRANDMA'S BALLS

Our grandmothers had some balls—and we don't mean any disrespect! Chicken liver and matzoh are the secret ingredients to this Jewish soul-food ball. The trick is coaxing all the sweet goodness from the onions. Well-browned onions in which the sugars are caramelized are the secret to many a Jewish dish, and here's where low and slow are key. You don't want them blackened or burned—as your grandma would say, "Have a little patience."

Makes about 2 dozen 1½-inch meatballs

5 TABLESPOONS OLIVE OIL

I ONION, FINELY DICED

½ CUP CHOPPED FRESH PARSLEY

¼ CUP KETCHUP

2 POUNDS 80% LEAN GROUND BEEF

¼ POUND CHICKEN LIVER, CHOPPED

2 SHEETS MATZOH, FINELY CRUMBLED

2 TEASPOONS SALT

¼ CUP BREAD CRUMBS

2 LARGE EGGS

✤ Preheat the oven to 450°F. Drizzle 2 tablespoons of the olive oil into a 9 × 13-inch baking dish and use your hand to evenly coat the entire surface. Set aside.

✤ Heat the remaining 3 tablespoons olive oil in a large frying pan over medium-high heat. Add the onions and stir frequently until they are well browned, but not burned, 8 to 10 minutes. Turn down the heat to low and allow the pan to cool for 3 minutes.

Add the parsley and ketchup, stirring to incorporate. Transfer the mixture to a small bowl and place in the refrigerator to cool.

✤ When the onion mixture is completely cool, combine it with the ground beef, chicken liver, matzoh, salt, bread crumbs, and eggs in a large mixing bowl and mix by hand until thoroughly incorporated.

✤ Roll the mixture into round, golf ball–size meatballs (about 1½ inches), making sure to pack the meat firmly. Place the balls in the prepared baking dish, being careful to line them up snugly and in even rows vertically and horizontally to form a grid. The meatballs should be touching one another.

✤ Roast for 20 minutes, or until the meatballs are firm and cooked through. A meat thermometer inserted into the center of a meatball should read 165°F.

✤ Allow the meatballs to cool for 5 minutes in the baking dish before serving.

THE BALLS

REUBEN BALLS

These balls represent the old-school deli soul of our Lower East Side neighborhood. When Jesse, one of the managers in the kitchen, brought up the idea of Reuben balls, we were a bit skeptical, but he insisted they would be delicious and asked if he could run a test batch. Well, he was clearly onto something because these balls taste just like a classic Reuben sandwich, especially when drizzled with Thousand Island Dressing (page 71). This is another meatball that works well in mini form as an hors d'oeuvre with dressing on the side for dipping.

Makes about thirty 1½-inch meatballs

2 TABLESPOONS OLIVE OIL

I POUND CORNED BEEF, FINELY DICED

I POUND GROUND PORK

1¼ CUPS SAUERKRAUT, ROUGHLY CHOPPED
AND SQUEEZED TO REMOVE AS MUCH LIQUID
AS POSSIBLE

5 LARGE EGGS

¾ POUND SWISS CHEESE, GRATED

2 SLICES FRESH RYE BREAD, FINELY DICED

I TEASPOON SALT

I TEASPOON CARAWAY SEEDS

✦ Preheat the oven to 450°F. Drizzle the olive oil into a 9 × 13-inch baking dish and use your hand to evenly coat the entire surface. Set aside.

✦ Combine the corned beef, ground pork, sauerkraut, eggs, Swiss cheese, bread, salt, and caraway seeds in a large mixing bowl and mix by hand until thoroughly incorporated.

✦ Roll the mixture into round, golf ball–size meatballs (about 1½ inches), making sure to pack the meat firmly. Place the balls in the prepared baking dish, being careful to line them up snugly and in even rows vertically and horizontally to form a grid. The meatballs should be touching one another.

✦ Roast for 20 minutes, or until the meatballs are firm and cooked through. A meat thermometer inserted into the center of a meatball should read 165°F.

✦ Allow the meatballs to cool for 5 minutes in the baking dish before serving.

P acked with jerk flavor and just the right amount of spice to keep you wanting more, these balls pair perfectly with sweet Mango Raisin Chutney (page 68). If you want to take the heat up a notch, add a pinch of cayenne pepper. Serve them over some fluffy white rice with Honey-Roasted Carrots with Prunes, Walnuts, and Mint (page 89). All that's left is to put on some Bob Marley and chill out with some friends and a cold Red Stripe.

Makes about 2 dozen 1½-inch meatballs

2 TABLESPOONS OLIVE OIL

I POUND GROUND CHICKEN, PREFERABLY THIGH MEAT

I POUND GROUND PORK

2 TABLESPOONS DARK BROWN SUGAR

I TEASPOON SALT

2 LARGE EGGS

2 HABANERO CHILES, STEMMED, SEEDED, AND MINCED

1½ TEASPOONS GROUND ALLSPICE

½ TEASPOON GROUND CINNAMON

½ TEASPOON GROUND CLOVES

¼ TEASPOON GROUND NUTMEG

¼ TEASPOON CAYENNE PEPPER (OPTIONAL)

2 TABLESPOONS CHOPPED FRESH THYME

3 SCALLIONS, THINLY SLICED

I TABLESPOON LOW-SODIUM SOY SAUCE

3 GARLIC CLOVES, MINCED

¾ CUP BREAD CRUMBS

✤ Preheat the oven to 450°F. Drizzle the olive oil into a 9 × 13-inch baking dish and use your hand to evenly coat the entire surface. Set aside.

✤ Combine the ground chicken, ground pork, brown sugar, salt, eggs, chiles, allspice, cinnamon, cloves, nutmeg, cayenne (if using), thyme, scallions, soy sauce, garlic, and bread crumbs in a large mixing bowl and mix by hand until thoroughly incorporated.

✤ Roll the mixture into round, golf ball–size meatballs (about 1½ inches), making sure to pack the meat firmly. Place the balls in the prepared baking dish, being careful to line them up snugly and in even rows vertically and horizontally to form a grid. The meatballs should be touching each other.

✤ Roast for 20 minutes, or until the meatballs are firm and cooked through. A meat thermometer inserted into the center of a meatball should read 165°F.

✤ Allow the meatballs to cool for 5 minutes in the baking dish before serving.

DUCK BALLS

The fancy, classic French flavors of duck a l'orange are showcased in this tasty ball. Because duck is one of the fattiest birds, it makes for especially tender meatballs. Ground duck may be hard to find, so ask your butcher to grind duck breasts and thighs, along with the skin. Serve with Sauce Vierge (page 65) or Mushroom Gravy (page 63).

Makes about 2 dozen 1½-inch meatballs

4 TABLESPOONS OLIVE OIL

I CUP FRESH ORANGE JUICE

I FENNEL HEAD, SLICED INTO ½-INCH-THICK
ROUNDS

2 POUNDS GROUND DUCK MEAT AND SKIN

2 LARGE EGGS

¾ CUP BREAD CRUMBS

2 SLICES FRESH WHITE BREAD, FINELY DICED
(ABOUT 1¾ CUPS)

2 TEASPOONS SALT

✤ Preheat the oven to 450°F. Drizzle 2 tablespoons of the olive oil into a 9 × 13-inch baking dish and use your hand to evenly coat the entire surface. Set aside.

✤ Bring the orange juice to a boil in a small pot over high heat and reduce by three-quarters, about 5 minutes. Set aside and allow to cool.

✤ Lay out the fennel rounds in a separate 9 × 13-inch baking dish. Drizzle with the remaining 2 tablespoons olive oil and ¼ cup water. Roast until soft, translucent, and beginning to brown, about 20 minutes. Place in the refrigerator to cool. Once they are cool, chop them finely.

✤ Combine the chopped fennel and reduced orange juice with the ground duck, eggs, bread crumbs, bread, and salt in a large mixing bowl and mix by hand until thoroughly incorporated.

✤ Roll the mixture into round, golf ball–size meatballs (about 1½ inches), making sure to pack the meat firmly. Place the balls in the prepared baking dish, being careful to line them up snugly and in even rows vertically and horizontally to form a grid. The meatballs should be touching one another.

✤ Roast for 20 minutes, or until the meatballs are firm and cooked through. A meat thermometer inserted into the center of a meatball should read 165°F.

✤ Allow the meatballs to cool for 5 minutes in the baking dish before serving.

STEAK 'N' BACON CHEDDAR BALLS

At the Shop we jokingly call these the heart-stoppers because while they are extremely rich and delicious, we wouldn't suggest eating them every day—which is tricky because once you try them, you won't stop craving them. Ready to really stop your heart? We have a "Family Jewels" option on the menu that allows guests to add a fried egg to any dish for a dollar. For our last meal, we would opt for steak 'n' bacon cheddar balls with a fried egg on top, served with Mushroom Gravy (page 63), and Creamed Spinach (page 100). For some added texture, ask your butcher to grind the beef more coarsely than usual; it gives the balls an added "steakiness."

Makes about 2 dozen 1½ inch balls

3 TABLESPOONS OLIVE OIL

1 ONION, FINELY DICED

8 OUNCES BACON, DICED (ABOUT 1½ CUPS)

2 POUNDS 80% LEAN GROUND BEEF

6 OUNCES CHEDDAR CHEESE, GRATED

3 LARGE EGGS

½ CUP BREAD CRUMBS

2 TEASPOONS SALT

✤ Preheat the oven to 450°F. Drizzle 2 tablespoons of the olive oil into a 9 × 13-inch baking dish and use your hand to evenly coat the entire surface. Set aside.

✤ Heat the remaining 1 tablespoon olive oil in a large frying pan over medium-high heat. Add the onions and bacon and cook, stirring frequently, until the bacon has browned and the onions are translucent, about 10 minutes. Using a slotted spoon, transfer the onions and bacon to a plate and place in the refrigerator to cool.

✤ Combine the ground beef, cheddar, eggs, bread crumbs, and salt in a large mixing bowl and mix by hand until thoroughly incorporated.

✤ Roll the mixture into round, golf ball–size meatballs (about 1½ inches), making sure to pack the meat firmly. Place the balls in the prepared baking dish, being careful to line them up snugly and in even rows vertically and horizontally to form a grid. The meatballs should be touching one another.

✤ Roast for 20 minutes, or until the meatballs are firm and cooked through. A meat thermometer inserted into the center of a meatball should read 165°F.

✤ Allow the meatballs to cool for 5 minutes in the baking dish before serving.

SALMON BALLS

his is our play on classic poached salmon. It's almost a croquette, and is perfect served with Lemon Cream Sauce (page 64) or with Classic Tomato Sauce (page 56) over spaghetti. If you prefer, try swapping freshly chopped dill for the tarragon, as it's also a natural partner with the salmon.

Makes about 2 dozen 1½-inch meatballs

4 TABLESPOONS OLIVE OIL

2 POUNDS SALMON FILLET, SKIN AND
BONES REMOVED

1 ONION, FINELY DICED

2 CELERY STALKS, FINELY DICED

½ CUP MAYONNAISE

2 LARGE EGGS

¾ CUP BREAD CRUMBS

¼ CUP CHOPPED FRESH PARSLEY

2 TABLESPOONS CHOPPED FRESH TARRAGON

2 TEASPOONS SALT

½ TEASPOON FRESHLY GROUND BLACK PEPPER

✤ Fill a large pot halfway with water and bring to a boil. Carefully lower the salmon into the pot. When the water comes back to a boil, turn off the heat and cover the pot with a tight-fitting lid. Allow the salmon to rest until it is just cooked through, about 10 minutes. Using a slotted spatula, transfer the salmon to a tray and place in the refrigerator to cool thoroughly, about 25 minutes.

✤ Preheat the oven to 450°F. Drizzle 2 tablespoons of the olive oil into a 9 × 13-inch baking dish and use your hand to evenly coat the entire surface. Set aside.

✤ Heat the remaining 2 tablespoons olive oil in a medium frying pan over medium-high heat. Add the onions and celery and cook, stirring frequently, until they are soft and translucent but not browned, about 10 minutes. Using a slotted spoon, transfer the vegetables to a tray and place in the refrigerator to cool.

✤ When the salmon and vegetables are completely cool, break the salmon into small pieces but do not completely shred. Combine the salmon and vegetables with the mayonnaise, eggs, bread crumbs, parsley, tarragon, salt, and pepper in a large mixing bowl and mix by hand until thoroughly incorporated.

✤ Roll the mixture into round, golf ball–size meatballs (about 1½ inches), making sure to pack the meat firmly. Place the balls in the prepared baking dish, being careful to line them up snugly and in even rows vertically and horizontally to form a grid. The meatballs should be touching one another.

✤ Roast for 15 minutes, or until the meatballs are firm and cooked through.

✤ Allow the meatballs to cool for 5 minutes in the baking dish before serving.

THE BALLS

DRUNKEN PORK BALLS

Don't mistake the recipe title for something you'd find at a frat party. This sophisticated ball came about when a friend brought us thirty pounds of wild boar from his hunting trip. Because that doesn't happen often, we switched to ground pork, and the balls are just as good. These meatballs are actually pretty simple, accented with a splash of Madeira, chopped rosemary and sage, and a hint of honey. Try to find a good-quality Madeira; it is reasonably inexpensive, and if you buy something decent, you can drink it with dinner. Serve these meatballs alongside one of the seasonal risottos (see pages 74 to 77), accompanied by Simple Arugula and Apple Salad (page 112).

Makes about 2 dozen 1½-inch meatballs

2 TABLESPOONS OLIVE OIL

2 POUNDS GROUND PORK SHOULDER

2 LARGE EGGS

2 SLICES FRESH WHITE BREAD, FINELY DICED
(ABOUT 1¾ CUPS)

¼ CUP BREAD CRUMBS

¼ CUP HONEY

½ CUP SWEET MADEIRA

2 TABLESPOONS CHOPPED FRESH ROSEMARY

2 TABLESPOONS CHOPPED FRESH SAGE

1 GARLIC CLOVE, MINCED

✤ Preheat the oven to 450°F. Drizzle the olive oil into a 9 × 13-inch baking dish and use your hand to evenly coat the entire surface. Set aside.

✤ Combine the ground pork, eggs, bread, bread crumbs, honey, Madeira, rosemary, sage, and garlic in a large mixing bowl and mix by hand until thoroughly incorporated.

✤ Roll the mixture into round, golf ball–size meatballs (about 1½ inches), making sure to pack the meat firmly. Place the balls in the prepared baking dish, being careful to line them up snugly and in even rows vertically and horizontally to form a grid. The meatballs should be touching one another.

✤ Roast for 20 minutes, or until the meatballs are firm and cooked through. A meat thermometer inserted into the center of a meatball should read 165°F.

✤ Allow the meatballs to cool for 5 minutes in the baking dish before serving.

BILLY GOAT BALLS

These meatballs were inspired by the ingredients often found in a goat cheese tart—pungent chevre, fresh thyme, and caramelized onions. Goat meat has a flavor a bit like lamb, but more gamier. Like most game meat, goat tends to be very lean, so it is important to add fat to avoid a dry meatball, and here the goat cheese delivers that fat, along with generous flavor. Try ground lamb if goat is unavailable. Serve these with Classic Tomato Sauce (page 56).

Makes about 2 dozen 1½-inch meatballs

4 TABLESPOONS OLIVE OIL

I ONION, CHOPPED

2 TEASPOONS SALT

I TABLESPOON FRESH THYME LEAVES

I TEASPOON SWEET PAPRIKA

¼ TEASPOON CRUSHED RED PEPPER FLAKES

½ CUP GOAT CHEESE

2 POUNDS GROUND GOAT MEAT

½ CUP BREAD CRUMBS

2 LARGE EGGS

✤ Preheat the oven to 450°F. Drizzle 2 tablespoons of the olive oil into a 9 × 13-inch baking dish and use your hand to evenly coat the entire surface. Set aside.

✤ Heat the remaining 2 tablespoons olive oil in a large frying pan over medium-high heat. Add the onions, 1 teaspoon of the salt, and the thyme. Lower the heat to medium and cook, stirring frequently, until the onions are soft and translucent, 10 to 15 minutes until nicely browned. Transfer to a bowl and place in the refrigerator to cool completely.

✤ Combine the cooled onion mixture with the paprika, red pepper flakes, goat cheese, ground goat meat, bread crumbs, and eggs in a large mixing bowl and mix by hand until thoroughly incorporated.

✤ Roll the mixture into round, golf ball–size meatballs (about 1½ inches), making sure to pack the meat firmly. Place the balls in the prepared baking dish, being careful to line them up snugly and in even rows vertically and horizontally to form a grid. The meatballs should be touching one another.

✤ Roast for 20 minutes, or until the meatballs are firm and cooked through. A meat thermometer inserted into the center of a meatball should read 165°F.

✤ Allow the meatballs to cool for 5 minutes in the baking dish before serving.

THE BALLS

SWEDISH MEATBALLS

C'mon, how could we not include this seventies' entertaining classic? But fear not, these aren't tired chafing-dish buffet standards; they are a delicious duo of beef and pork, along with a well-spiced mixture of allspice and mustard powder and a touch of heavy cream. While people may argue over authenticity, we're not Swedish, but we know these are darn good. Serve them with our Mushroom Gravy (page 63), Mashed Potatoes (page 79), and a bit of lingonberry jam.

Makes about 2 dozen 1½-inch meatballs

2 TABLESPOONS OLIVE OIL

3 SLICES FRESH WHITE BREAD, ROUGHLY TORN

½ CUP BEEF BROTH

½ CUP HEAVY CREAM

2 TABLESPOONS UNSALTED BUTTER

I ONION, FINELY DICED

2 TABLESPOONS CHOPPED FRESH PARSLEY

¼ TEASPOON GROUND ALLSPICE

¼ TEASPOON DRY MUSTARD POWDER

2 TABLESPOONS ALL-PURPOSE FLOUR

I POUND 80% LEAN GROUND BEEF

I POUND GROUND PORK SHOULDER

2 TEASPOONS SALT

½ TEASPOON FRESHLY GROUND BLACK PEPPER

2 LARGE EGGS

✢ Preheat the oven to 450°F. Drizzle the olive oil into a 9 × 13-inch baking dish and use your hand to evenly coat the entire surface. Set aside.

✢ Place the torn bread, beef broth, and cream in a bowl and let soak for 5 minutes

✢ Melt the butter in a frying pan over medium-high heat. Add the onions and cook, stirring frequently, until transparent, 6 to 8 minutes. Add the parsley, allspice, mustard powder, and flour and stir to incorporate. Pour the contents of the pan into the bowl with the bread mixture and stir until well mixed. Set aside to cool.

✢ Combine the cooled onion and bread mixture with the ground beef, ground pork, salt, pepper, and eggs in a large mixing bowl and mix by hand until thoroughly incorporated.

✢ Roll the mixture into round, golf ball–size meatballs (about 1½ inches), making sure to pack the meat firmly. Place the balls in the prepared baking dish, being careful to line them up snugly and in even rows vertically and horizontally to form a grid. The meatballs should be touching one another.

✢ Roast for 20 minutes, or until the meatballs are firm and cooked through. A meat thermometer inserted into the center of a meatball should read 165°F.

✢ Allow the meatballs to cool for 5 minutes in the baking dish before serving.

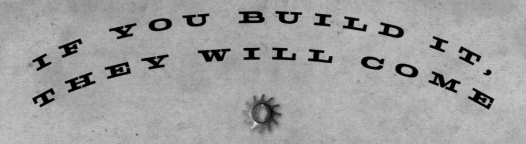

IF YOU BUILD IT, THEY WILL COME

A MEATBALL SANDWICH BAR

There's something unbelievably gratifying about holding a warm meatball sandwich between your hands and anticipating that first awesome bite. A build-your-own-meatball-hero bar is a great and easy way to entertain because it taps into the make-it-your-own customization that is our credo at the Shop. Plus it's a super easy way to entertain because almost everything can be done ahead of time. The fun factor comes from letting everyone mix and match his or her ultimate sandwich. We suggest you make two or three different balls and arrange them on the stove or on prewarmed platters; set sliced rolls and a variety of cheeses, like sliced provolone and mozzarella, alongside. Also offer two or three favorite sauces such as Spicy Meat Sauce (page 57), Spinach-Basil Pesto (page 58), and Parmesan Cream Sauce (page 60) for spreading between the bread and balls. Have some aluminum foil–lined sheet pans ready to go and the broiler on high for bubbling melted cheese. We like to offer a few sides, like our Creamy Polenta (page 78), Mashed Potatoes (page 79), Roasted Fennel with Raisins, Walnuts, and Parsley (page 91), Roasted Cauliflower with Hot Cherry Peppers and Bread Crumbs (page 97), and any of our salads, like our Simple Arugula and Apple Salad (page 112) or the Romaine, Cucumber, and Tomato Salad (page 119). For dessert, really go for it and have a couple flavors of ice cream set out with individual scoops alongside baskets of different home-baked cookies ready to pair up so you can finish the night off with the perfect ice-cream sandwich.

GOBBLE GOBBLE BALLS

All the flavors of our favorite holiday in the perfect package. Ground turkey, stuffing, dried cranberries, plus a pinch of homey cinnamon come together for a fall favorite with none of the fuss. While roast turkey can often be dry, these balls stay nice and moist. Serve these as minis for an hors d'oeuvre or for a cozy Sunday-night meal paired with Roasted Brussels Sprouts with Apples and Honey-Roasted Pecans (page 90) and Candied Yams (page 82).

Makes about 2 dozen 1½-inch meatballs

2 TABLESPOONS OLIVE OIL

2 POUNDS GROUND TURKEY

2 CUPS GARLIC CROUTONS (PAGE 119) OR STUFFING CUBES

1 CUP DRIED CRANBERRIES

2 LARGE EGGS

¼ CUP BREAD CRUMBS

2 TABLESPOONS CHOPPED FRESH SAGE

2 TEASPOONS SALT

PINCH OF GROUND CINNAMON

✣ Preheat the oven to 450°F. Drizzle the olive oil into a 9 × 13-inch baking dish and use your hand to evenly coat the entire surface. Set aside.

✣ Combine the ground turkey, croutons, cranberries, eggs, bread crumbs, sage, salt, and cinnamon in a large mixing bowl and mix by hand until thoroughly incorporated.

✣ Roll the mixture into round, golf ball–size meatballs (about 1½ inches), making sure to pack the meat firmly. Place the balls in the prepared baking dish, being careful to line them up snugly and in even rows vertically and horizontally to form a grid. The meatballs should be touching one another.

✣ Roast for 20 minutes, or until the meatballs are firm and cooked through. A meat thermometer inserted into the center of a meatball should read 165°F.

✣ Allow the meatballs to cool for 5 minutes in the baking dish before serving.

THE BALLS

TANDOORI LAMB BALLS

Travel the globe and you'll discover that every culture has a meatball. These balls highlight the exotic flavors and all the goodness from the great tandoor ovens of India. At the Shop we serve these with our simple Cilantro Yogurt Sauce (page 69), which is cool and refreshing and the perfect complement to the spice-rich tandoori flavor. This recipe also works really well with ground chicken or beef.

Makes about 2 dozen 1½-inch balls

2 TABLESPOONS OLIVE OIL

2 POUNDS GROUND LAMB

½ CUP BREAD CRUMBS

2 LARGE EGGS

I CUP CHOPPED FRESH CILANTRO
(INCLUDING STEMS)

JUICE FROM I LEMON

¼ CUP TANDOORI SPICE MIX (RECIPE FOLLOWS)

2 TEASPOONS SALT

✤ Preheat the oven to 450°F. Drizzle the olive oil into a 9 × 13-inch baking dish and use your hand to evenly coat the entire surface. Set aside.

✤ Combine the ground lamb, bread crumbs, eggs, cilantro, lemon juice, tandoori spice mix, and salt in a large mixing bowl and mix by hand until thoroughly incorporated.

✤ Roll the mixture into round, golf ball–size meatballs (about 1½ inches), making sure to pack the meat firmly. Place the balls in the prepared baking dish, being careful to line them up snugly and in even rows vertically and horizontally to form a grid. The meatballs should be touching one another.

✤ Roast for 20 minutes, or until the meatballs are firm and cooked through. A meat thermometer inserted into the center of a meatball should read 165°F.

✤ Allow the meatballs to cool for 5 minutes in the baking dish before serving.

TANDOORI SPICE MIX

2 TEASPOONS GROUND GINGER

2 TEASPOONS GROUND CUMIN

2 TEASPOONS GROUND CORIANDER

2 TEASPOONS SWEET PAPRIKA

2 TEASPOONS GROUND TURMERIC

2 TEASPOONS CAYENNE PEPPER

Mix together the ginger, cumin, coriander, paprika, turmeric, and cayenne in a bowl. This spice mix will keep in an airtight container for up to 6 months.

THE BALLS

VENISON, AKA BAMBI, BALLS

A friend of ours is a hunter, and we created this ball after he brought us back the goods from a successful outing. It's based on a classic Cumberland sauce, and we've added a touch of chocolate and butter to add richness and the extra fat that the lean and gamy venison requires. Venison is typically paired with juniper berries, which we like to crush and mix in along with a splash of port wine. Serve with Mushroom Gravy (page 68) and Smashed Turnips with Fresh Horseradish (page 80).

Makes about 2 dozen 1½-inch meatballs

2 TABLESPOONS OLIVE OIL

8 TABLESPOONS (1 STICK) UNSALTED BUTTER

4 OUNCES BITTERSWEET CHOCOLATE

2 POUNDS GROUND VENISON

½ CUP PORT WINE

4 JUNIPER BERRIES, FINELY CRUSHED

1 GARLIC CLOVE, MINCED

2 SLICES FRESH WHITE BREAD, FINELY DICED
(ABOUT 1¾ CUPS)

¼ CUP BREAD CRUMBS

2 LARGE EGGS

✤ Preheat the oven to 450°F. Drizzle the olive oil into a 9 × 13-inch baking dish and use your hand to evenly coat the entire surface. Set aside.

✤ Combine the butter and chocolate in the top of a double boiler and melt over medium heat. Remove from the heat and allow the chocolate to cool so that it is just warm, but still in liquid form.

✤ Combine the chocolate mixture with the ground venison, port wine, juniper berries, garlic, bread, bread crumbs, and eggs in a large mixing bowl and mix by hand until thoroughly incorporated.

✤ Roll the mixture into round, golf ball–size meatballs (about 1½ inches), making sure to pack the meat firmly. Place the balls in the prepared baking dish, being careful to line them up snugly and in even rows vertically and horizontally to form a grid. The meatballs should be touching one another.

✤ Roast for 20 minutes, or until the meatballs are firm and cooked through. A meat thermometer inserted into the center of a meatball should read 165°F.

✤ Allow the meatballs to cool for 5 minutes in the baking dish before serving.

THE 10 COMMANDMENTS

OF A GREAT SANDWICH

SEEMINGLY SIMPLE, YET ONE OF THE HARDEST DISHES TO BUILD.
For a meatball hero, while it's definitely all about the balls, it is also about the interplay between the best Italian bread, the smoothness of the mozzarella, or the tang of the provolone. Complement and contrast—these are the most important things for the perfect sandwich. Here are some guidelines to help you along the way to concocting the perfect bite for any sandwich.

1. IT'S ALL ABOUT THE RATIO. Bread, main ingredient, garnish, and sauce—too much or too little of any ingredient can ruin the ultimate sandwich.

2. THE BREAD CAN MAKE OR BREAK A SANDWICH. It should never be treated as an afterthought. Remember, unless you are serving a sandwich open-faced, there will be two pieces of bread, and very often too much bread is the culprit in a poorly balanced sandwich. Try slicing loaf bread thinly or hollowing out a baguette. Choose a bread that is crusty on the outside and soft on the inside. Or try focaccia.

3. SPREAD THE SAUCE ALL OVER. The first and last bites are the most memorable, so whatever the sauce (mayo, tomato sauce, butter, etc.), spread it evenly and make sure it reaches the edges of the bread. A dry first bite can be ruinous.

4. BUILD IT TO FIT IN YOUR MOUTH. It's fun to get a huge sandwich, but in the end, if it doesn't fit in your mouth, you can't eat it. Two and one-half inches is the maximum height allowance for any great sandwich.

5. **IF IT FALLS APART, IT AIN'T A SANDWICH ANYMORE.** Build a sandwich like an engineer: stable from the first bite to the last. For example, juicy tomatoes can make the filling of a sandwich slippery. Be sure to put them on the very top, just underneath the bread, not underneath the meat, where they will tend to slide.

6. **SOGGY AIN'T SEXY.** For a sandwich with a saucy sauce like a meatball hero, make sure your bread will stand up to the challenge. A good, crusty Italian bread will usually do the trick. Remember that fat repels water, so if you're using sliced bread, which tends to sop up the sauce, add a thin layer of butter or mayonnaise to help to slow down the sogginess or moisture migration.

7. **TOO MUCH MEAT CAN BE INTIMIDATING.** The meat is just one of the ingredients; it should be the highlight, not the only thing you taste.

8. **TEXTURE RULES.** Crispy, crunchy, supple, soft, and moist. A great sandwich will fire on all textural cylinders. Keep this in mind when planning your ingredients and build your sandwich accordingly.

9. **TEMPERATURE IS KEY.** No one likes icy cold cuts, and no one enjoys being burned by an overly hot sauce. A ravenous eater should be able to tear into a sandwich without remorse. Be aware of the time between construction and consumption: A saucy hero will be cold and soggy if not eaten right away. Choose a sandwich for the occasion and time frame.

10. **WHEN IN DOUBT, LEAVE IT OUT.** A great sandwich is a work of art, and an artist knows when enough is enough. So while we urge you to be creative and unafraid to try something different (interesting ingredients like potato chips can add crunch) also know when to rein it in.

THAI BALLS

A few months after the Shop opened we got a call from the Food Network asking if we would be interested in being guests on *Big Daddy's House* with host Aaron McCargo, Jr. They asked if we could develop a new meatball for their Thai-themed episode. The recipe, which captures all of the fresh, wonderful flavors of Southeast Asia, was a big hit on the show and in the Shop as well. Be careful not to chop the herbs too finely and feel free to add extra chiles if you prefer your meatballs extra spicy. The garnish—crunchy peanuts, basil, and grated carrots hit with rice wine vinegar and soy sauce—is a killer. Serve it all with Peanut Sauce (page 67, optional).

Makes about 2 dozen 1½-inch balls

2 TABLESPOONS OLIVE OIL

I POUND GROUND PORK

I POUND SHRIMP, SHELLED, DEVEINED, AND
ROUGHLY CHOPPED

2 LARGE EGGS

¾ CUP FRESH THAI OR ITALIAN BASIL,
ROUGHLY CHOPPED

¾ CUP FRESH CILANTRO, ROUGHLY CHOPPED

½ CUP FRESH MINT, ROUGHLY CHOPPED

2 THAI CHILES, STEMMED, SEEDED, AND MINCED

½ CUP BREAD CRUMBS

2 TABLESPOONS MINCED LEMONGRASS OR
LEMONGRASS PASTE

2 TABLESPOONS MINCED FRESH GINGER

2 GARLIC CLOVES, MINCED

JUICE FROM I LIME

2 TABLESPOONS LOW-SODIUM SOY SAUCE

2 TABLESPOONS SESAME SEEDS

2 TABLESPOONS FISH SAUCE

FOR THE GARNISH

I TEASPOON RICE WINE VINEGAR

I TEASPOON LOW-SODIUM SOY SAUCE

2 LARGE CARROTS, JULIENNED OR GRATED USING
THE LARGE HOLES OF A BOX GRATER

IO FRESH THAI BASIL OR ITALIAN BASIL LEAVES,
ROUGHLY CHOPPED

¼ CUP ROUGHLY CHOPPED FRESH CILANTRO
(INCLUDING STEMS)

IO FRESH MINT LEAVES, ROUGHLY CHOPPED

¼ CUP ROASTED PEANUTS, CHOPPED

I TEASPOON SESAME SEEDS

✤ Preheat the oven to 450°F. Drizzle the olive oil into a 9 × 13-inch baking dish and use your hand to evenly coat the entire surface. Set aside.

(Continued on page 47)

✦ Combine the ground pork, shrimp, eggs, basil, cilantro, mint, chiles, bread crumbs, lemongrass, ginger, garlic, lime juice, soy sauce, sesame seeds, and fish sauce in a large mixing bowl and mix by hand until thoroughly incorporated.

✦ Roll the mixture into round, golf ball–size meatballs (about 1½ inches), making sure to pack the meat firmly. Place the balls in the prepared baking dish, being careful to line them up snugly and in even rows vertically and horizontally to form a grid. The meatballs should be touching one another.

✦ Roast for 20 minutes, or until the meatballs are firm and cooked through. A meat thermometer inserted into the center of a meatball should read 165°F.

✦ Allow the meatballs to cool for 5 minutes in the baking dish.

✦ Meanwhile, to make the garnish, place the rice wine vinegar, soy sauce, carrots, basil, cilantro, mint, peanuts, and sesame seeds in a bowl and toss to combine.

✦ Spoon the garnish over the top of the meatballs and serve with the peanut sauce (if using).

VEAL MEATBALLS

With its rich and subtle flavor, veal is one of the traditional meats used in Italian meatballs. Here we layer it with Parmesan cheese, oregano, and aromatic vegetables. At the Shop we use veal breast, which is inexpensive and has a relatively high fat content. It is a bit more work to butcher and grind, but it's worth the exceptional outcome. Ask your butcher in advance to bone the breast and grind it for you. Serve with Sauce Vierge (page 65) and Braised Green Beans (page 101).

Makes about 2 dozen 1½-inch meatballs

3 TABLESPOONS OLIVE OIL

I LARGE ONION, FINELY DICED (ABOUT 2 CUPS)

2 TEASPOONS SALT

2 POUNDS GROUND VEAL

3 LARGE EGGS

⅔ CUP BREAD CRUMBS

¼ CUP GRATED PARMESAN CHEESE

I CARROT, FINELY DICED (ABOUT I CUP)

I CELERY STALK, FINELY DICED

¼ CUP CHOPPED FRESH PARSLEY

I TABLESPOON CHOPPED FRESH OREGANO
OR I TEASPOON DRIED

½ TEASPOON FRESHLY GROUND BLACK PEPPER

✤ Preheat the oven to 450°F. Drizzle 2 tablespoons of the olive oil into a 9 × 13-inch baking dish and use your hand to evenly coat the entire surface. Set aside.

✤ Heat the remaining 1 tablespoon olive oil in a large frying pan over high heat. Add the onions and salt. Cook, stirring frequently until the onions just start to turn translucent and begin to brown, about 3 minutes. Using a slotted spoon, transfer them to a plate and place in the refrigerator to cool.

✤ Combine the cooled onions with the ground veal, eggs, bread crumbs, Parmesan, carrots, celery, parsley, oregano, and pepper in a large mixing bowl and mix by hand until thoroughly incorporated.

✤ Roll the mixture into round, golf ball–size meatballs (about 1½ inches), making sure to pack the meat firmly. Place the balls in the prepared baking dish, being careful to line them up snugly and in even rows vertically and horizontally to form a grid. The meatballs should be touching one another.

✤ Roast for 20 minutes, or until the meatballs are firm and cooked through. A meat thermometer inserted into the center of a meatball should read 165°F.

✤ Allow the meatballs to cool for 5 minutes in the baking dish before serving.

MEET YOUR BUTCHER

While you can pretty much find most of the meats you'll need for the meatballs in the refrigerated meat section at your market, we heartily suggest stopping by your local butcher's counter and having your meat custom-ground. We know you may have seen this suggestion in many a cookbook. But a relationship with your butcher is definitely worth cultivating, especially when it comes to meatballs. Butchers are filled with great advice, and they can be the go-to guys (or gals) when it comes to some of the recipes, like the Duck Balls (page 31), that we've created. Some recipes include offbeat or forgotten cuts like breast of veal, but a good butcher may actually be happy that you're checking out some unsung heroes and straying from the usual ground chuck. You might want to call ahead, as some of the cuts may need special ordering—the rabbit for our Bunny Balls (page 50), for example. By all means, pull out your own meat grinder, but if you're not up for it, we hope you'll reconnect with your butcher and try some of the more under-the-usual-radar recipes. Also, some supermarkets still do their own butchering and grinding, so stop by (preferably not during the six p.m. after-work rush) and ask if they will custom-grind your meat for you.

We created these balls in honor of Easter. We won't lie to you—they are a serious undertaking, and are without a doubt the most complicated recipe in this book. *But* we promise that the end result is completely worth the effort. Braising the legs with the onion and thyme brings out their incredible flavor and tenderness. Butchering the rabbit can prove a bit tricky, so visit your local butcher shop at an off-hour when the butchers have some extra time on their hands to help you. Serve with Mushroom Gravy (page 63) and Mashed Potatoes (page 79).

Makes about 2 dozen 1½-inch meatballs

4 TABLESPOONS OLIVE OIL

I ONION, CUT INTO ¼-INCH SLICES

I FENNEL HEAD, CUT INTO ¼-INCH SLICES

2 TEASPOONS SALT

TWO 2-POUND RABBITS (FRONT AND HIND
LEGS SEPARATED, LOIN DEBONED,
AND LOIN AND BELLY GROUND)

2 TABLESPOONS CHOPPED FRESH ROSEMARY

½ TEASPOON FRESHLY GROUND BLACK PEPPER

I GARLIC CLOVE, MINCED

¼ CUP DRY WHITE WINE

I CUP CHOPPED FRESH PARSLEY

2 LARGE EGGS

I CUP BREAD CRUMBS

✤ Preheat the oven to 375°F. Drizzle 2 tablespoons of the olive oil into a 9 × 13-inch baking dish and use your hand to evenly coat the entire surface. Set aside.

✤ Heat the remaining 2 tablespoons olive oil in a large frying pan for 1 minute over medium-high heat. Add the onions, fennel, and salt. Cook, stirring often, until the vegetables are tender and begin to brown, about 10 minutes.

✤ Place the rabbit legs in another baking dish and cover with the hot onion mixture. Roast for 1 hour and 15 minutes, turning the legs every 10 minutes. When done, the meat should be tender and falling off the bone.

✤ Remove from the oven and allow to cool. Pick the cooked meat off the bones, being careful to remove all of the bones. Coarsely chop the meat, combine with the onion mixture, and set aside.

✤ Raise the oven temperature to 450°F.

✤ Combine the cooked, chopped rabbit mixture with the raw ground rabbit, rosemary, pepper, garlic, white wine, parsley, eggs, and bread crumbs in a large mixing bowl and mix by hand until thoroughly incorporated.

(Continued on next page)

✦ Roll the mixture into round, golf ball–size meatballs (about 1½ inches), making sure to pack the meat firmly. Place the balls in the prepared baking dish, being careful to line them up snugly and in even rows vertically and horizontally to form a grid. The meatballs should be touching each other.

✦ Roast for 20 minutes, or until the meatballs are firm and cooked through. A meat thermometer inserted into the center of a meatball should read 165°F.

✦ Allow the meatballs to cool for 5 minutes in the baking dish before serving.

CHAPTER

THE SAUCES

"FROTH NOT, DO NOT RAISE THE LID OF THE CAULDRON;
SIMMER WELL, AND BE PATIENT, FOR I AM COOKING YOU."
—RUMI

CLASSIC TOMATO SAUCE

Since everyone has his or her version of this sauce, we spent *a lot* of time getting this one right. No surprise, the best results came from using the best ingredients. When it comes to tomato sauce, using poor-quality canned tomatoes can leave an acidic or tinny taste in your mouth. So while it is a bit more expensive, we like to use Pomi brand chopped tomatoes (you know, the ones that come in the box). The sauce starts with a careful "sweating" of onions (cooking them slowly, until translucent but not brown, to extract as much flavor as possible), and the flavor continues to build from a nice, long, low-heat simmering after the tomatoes are added.

Makes 7 cups

¼ CUP OLIVE OIL

I ONION, FINELY DICED

I BAY LEAF

I TEASPOON CHOPPED FRESH OREGANO OR

½ TEASPOON DRIED

2 GARLIC CLOVES, ROUGHLY CHOPPED

2 TEASPOONS SALT OR TO TASTE

2 TABLESPOONS TOMATO PASTE

TWO 26-OUNCE BOXES POMI CHOPPED TOMATOES

OR TWO 28-OUNCE CANS WHOLE PLUM

TOMATOES, CHOPPED WITH THEIR LIQUID

✤ Heat the olive oil in a large pot over medium heat. Add the onions, bay leaf, oregano, garlic, and salt and cook, stirring often, until the onions are soft and translucent, about 10 minutes.

✤ Add the tomato paste and continue cooking for 5 minutes. Add the tomatoes and stir constantly until the sauce begins to boil. Lower the heat and simmer for 1 hour, stirring every 5 minutes or so to prevent the sauce on the bottom of the pot from burning. Taste and season with additional salt, if desired. Remove the bay leaf before serving.

SPICY MEAT SAUCE

We hate to choose favorites—we love all our "children" equally—but this sauce is the one we go to again and again and again. It has the perfect amount of kick to it, but if you prefer it spicier, feel free to add more red pepper flakes. But please—this is a big tip coming—wait a minute or two after you've added the red pepper flakes before adding more. Give the peppers some time to hydrate and the spice to dissolve—a little chile goes a long way but takes time before it reaches its full potential. Of course we love this sauce over pasta and on a Smash (two balls on a brioche roll with sauce and cheese) too. Try tossing in a handful of arugula with the hot pasta and sauce and allowing it to wilt, adding a generous grating of Parmesan cheese on top. Perfection!

Makes 8 cups

2 TABLESPOONS OLIVE OIL

I LARGE ONION, FINELY DICED

I POUND GROUND PORK, PREFERABLY SHOULDER

2 TEASPOONS CRUSHED RED PEPPER FLAKES

2 TEASPOONS SALT OR TO TASTE

2 TABLESPOONS TOMATO PASTE

TWO 26-OUNCE BOXES POMI CHOPPED TOMATOES
OR TWO 28-OUNCE CANS WHOLE
PLUM TOMATOES, ROUGHLY CHOPPED
WITH THEIR LIQUID

✦ Heat the olive oil in a large pot over medium heat. Add the onions, ground pork, red pepper flakes, and salt and cook, stirring constantly, until the meat is thoroughly cooked and the onions are soft and beginning to brown, about 15 minutes.

✦ Add the tomato paste and continue cooking for 5 minutes. Add the tomatoes and stir constantly until the sauce begins to boil. Continue cooking for 35 minutes, stirring every 5 minutes or so to prevent the sauce on the bottom of the pot from burning. Taste and season with additional salt, if desired.

SPINACH-BASIL PESTO

This pesto is very simple, and its mild, herbaceous flavor makes it the ideal companion for just about any of the meatballs. While many pesto recipes call for pine nuts, we prefer the flavor (and lower price) of walnuts. Try finely chopping them and adding them right at the end for a nice, crunchy texture. We also love this as a healthy party dip, especially because it has no raw garlic—your guests will thank you too! Just cut up some carrots, cherry tomatoes, bell peppers, and celery and you're ready to go. You can swap arugula for spinach if you prefer. Pesto freezes well and will keep for up to three months in the freezer.

Makes 4 cups

¼ CUP ROUGHLY CHOPPED WALNUTS

4 CUPS BABY SPINACH LEAVES

2 CUPS FRESH BASIL

I TEASPOON SALT OR TO TASTE

½ CUP OLIVE OIL

¼ CUP GRATED PARMESAN CHEESE

✤ Preheat the oven to 350°F.

✤ Fill a large stockpot three-quarters full with water and bring to a boil over high heat.

✤ Meanwhile, spread out the walnuts on a small rimmed baking sheet and roast in the oven for about 12 minutes, giving them a shake after 6 minutes. Continue roasting until golden brown and toasted. Set aside and allow to cool thoroughly.

✤ Fill a large bowl halfway with ice and water, and set it close to the sink.

✤ Dump the spinach and basil into the boiling water and stir. After 1 minute, strain the greens, and plunge them into the bowl with ice water. Drain the greens again and squeeze them tightly to get as much water out as possible. Chop the greens roughly.

✤ Combine the greens and walnuts with the salt, olive oil, and Parmesan in a food processor and process until a smooth consistency is reached. Taste and season with additional salt, if desired.

PARMESAN CREAM SAUCE

Now this is the stuff. Rich beyond your wildest dreams, this sauce is not for the faint of heart. We think of it as Alfredo sauce on steroids, and it's worth every calorie! At the Shop it's a must-order with Chicken Meatballs (page 12). There's pretty much nothing a ladle of this creamy sauce can't improve—stir it into sautéed spinach for instant Creamed Spinach (page 100), or spoon it over steamed cauliflower, top with Parmesan cheese, and bake in the oven for the perfect gratin.

Makes 4 cups

1 WHOLE HEAD GARLIC

2 CUPS WHOLE MILK

2 CUPS HEAVY CREAM

¼ CUP DRY WHITE WINE

½ BUNCH FRESH THYME

2 TEASPOONS SALT

2 TABLESPOONS UNSALTED BUTTER, SOFTENED

2 TABLESPOONS ALL-PURPOSE FLOUR

½ TEASPOON FRESHLY GROUND BLACK PEPPER

¼ CUP GRATED PARMESAN CHEESE

✢ Cut the head of garlic in half horizontally. Reserve one half for another use.

✢ Place the milk, cream, white wine, garlic half, thyme, and salt in a large saucepan and bring to a boil over medium-high heat, stirring occasionally so as not to scald the milk. Watch the mixture closely so that it does not boil over. Once the cream has come to a boil, immediately reduce the heat to its lowest setting and let the mixture simmer slowly for 45 minutes.

✢ In the meantime, combine the butter and flour in a small bowl and mix together with the back of a wooden spoon until a smooth paste forms.

✢ Add the paste to the cream sauce and whisk continuously until the paste has completely dissolved and the sauce has thickened. Remove the sauce from the heat and whisk in the pepper and Parmesan. Strain the sauce through a fine-mesh sieve and serve.

L.E.S. BARBECUE SAUCE

Sure, you can buy barbecue sauce, but wait until you try ours—it's what we call QC, or quick cook. You probably already have most of the ingredients in your fridge or pantry. This tangy Lower East Side creation is the star ingredient in our BBQ Pork Balls (page 11), but it shines on its own with any grilled meat or bird.

Makes 3 cups

2 TABLESPOONS OLIVE OIL

1 ONION, FINELY DICED

6 GARLIC CLOVES, ROUGHLY CHOPPED

1 TABLESPOON GROUND CUMIN

½ TEASPOON CRUSHED RED PEPPER FLAKES

2 TEASPOONS SALT

¼ CUP (2 OUNCES) BREWED ESPRESSO OR
1 TEASPOON INSTANT ESPRESSO POWDER
DISSOLVED IN 2 OUNCES BOILING WATER

½ CUP APPLE CIDER VINEGAR

¼ CUP WHISKEY

2 CUPS KETCHUP

1½ CUPS FIRMLY PACKED DARK BROWN SUGAR

✤ Heat the olive oil in a saucepan over medium heat. Add the onions, garlic, cumin, red pepper flakes, and salt and cook stirring frequently, until the onions are soft and translucent and the garlic is soft, about 10 minutes. Do not allow the garlic to brown (add a few tablespoons of water, if necessary, to prevent browning).

✤ Add the espresso, vinegar, and whiskey and bring to a boil. Remove from the heat and transfer the mixture to a blender. Blend on high until smooth. Return the mixture to the pan and whisk in the ketchup and brown sugar until fully incorporated and smooth.

MUSHROOM GRAVY

This gravy is so good you may just end up eating it like soup, spoonful after spoonful. We ladle it over practically any meatball in this book, and we also really love it over a big steaming bowl of Mashed Potatoes (page 79). You can make it ahead, though be careful to stir it frequently while reheating, scraping up the sauce on the bottom of the saucepan to avoid burning.

Makes 4 cups

¼ CUP OLIVE OIL

I LARGE ONION, HALVED AND CUT INTO ⅛-INCH SLICES

I½ TABLESPOONS SALT

I TABLESPOON FRESH THYME

I POUND BUTTON MUSHROOMS, WIPED CLEAN AND CUT INTO ¼-INCH SLICES

⅔ CUP DRY WHITE WINE

4 CUPS CHICKEN STOCK

4 TABLESPOONS (½ STICK) UNSALTED BUTTER

¼ CUP ALL-PURPOSE FLOUR

⅓ CUP CHOPPED FRESH PARSLEY

FRESHLY GROUND BLACK PEPPER

✤ Heat the olive oil in a large saucepan over medium heat. Add the onions, salt, and thyme and cook, stirring constantly, until the onions have become soft and translucent, about 10 minutes.

✤ Add the mushrooms and cook until almost all of their liquid has evaporated, about 10 minutes. Add the white wine and continue cooking until the pan is almost dry, about 5 minutes. Add the chicken stock and continue cooking until the stock is reduced by half, about 30 minutes.

✤ In the meantime, combine the butter and flour in a small bowl and mix together with the back of a wooden spoon until a smooth paste forms. Add the paste to the simmering gravy and whisk continuously until the paste has completely dissolved and the gravy has thickened. Stir in the parsley and add pepper to taste.

LEMON CREAM SAUCE

Once you taste this fast and easy go-to sauce, we're willing to bet it will become a staple in your kitchen for any fish or chicken dish. The lemon brightens the roasted flavor of meatballs like Salmon Balls (page 34), Bouillabaisse Balls (page 23), and Chicken Meatballs (page 12). Drizzle it over braised greens or sautéed spinach for a big impact with little fuss.

Makes 2 cups

1 CUP HEAVY CREAM

1 CUP SOUR CREAM

JUICE FROM ½ LEMON

¾ TEASPOOON SALT OR TO TASTE

FRESHLY GROUND BLACK PEPPER

✤ Heat the cream in a small saucepan over medium-high heat and bring to a boil. Lower the heat and whisk in the sour cream. Heat gently just until warm; do not allow to boil. Remove from the heat and whisk in the lemon juice, salt, and pepper to taste.

THE SAUCES

SAUCE VIERGE

We've revived this simple, classic French sauce with a combination of extra-virgin olive oil, tomatoes, fresh herbs, and some toasted pine nuts. It's a summertime sauce that's typically served with fish, but we like it with many of the meatballs, including Duck Balls (page 31) and Veal Meatballs (page 48). On a hot summer day meatballs can be dauntingly heavy, and a bright, fresh sauce can turn them into a suprisingly light lunch. Since chervil can be tricky to find, feel free to skip it if you can't find it.

Makes 4 cups

4 RIPE BEEFSTEAK TOMATOES, FINELY DICED

I SMALL RED ONION, FINELY DICED

½ CUP PINE NUTS, TOASTED

½ CUP EXTRA-VIRGIN OLIVE OIL

JUICE FROM 2 LEMONS

I CUP CHOPPED FRESH CILANTRO

¼ CUP THINLY SLICED FRESH CHIVES

¼ CUP CHOPPED FRESH PARSLEY

¼ CUP CHOPPED FRESH CHERVIL (OPTIONAL)

¼ CUP CHOPPED FRESH BASIL

I TABLESPOON SALT OR TO TASTE

✤ Place the tomatoes, onions, pine nuts, olive oil, lemon juice, cilantro, chives, parsley, chervil (if using), basil, and salt in a large bowl and mix until thoroughly combined. Taste and adjust the seasoning, if desired.

SALSA ROJA

The fresh punch of tomatoes, cilantro, and lime makes this sauce a natural fit for Viva la México Balls (page 27), but try it as a dip with chips too. This sauce will keep for up to four days in the fridge.

Makes 4 cups

2 15-OUNCE CANS CHOPPED TOMATOES WITH
GREEN CHILES

3 FRESH JALAPEÑO PEPPERS, STEMMED, SEEDED,
AND FINELY CHOPPED

1 SMALL ONION, FINELY CHOPPED

JUICE FROM 1 LIME

¼ CUP MINCED FRESH CILANTRO

1 TEASPOON SALT OR TO TASTE

3 DASHES TABASCO SAUCE

✤ Place the tomatoes, jalapeños, onions, lime juice, cilantro, salt, and Tabasco sauce in a large bowl and mix until thoroughly combined. Taste and adjust the seasoning, if desired.

THE SAUCES

PEANUT SAUCE

Addictive and easy, this is our version of a quick Asian-inspired sauce that we serve with Thai Balls (page 45). However, we also think it's a smashing success alongside fresh-cut veggies as a crudités dipping sauce. Alternatively, try mixing a few tablespoons in with your next stir-fry or thinning it with water and serving it over Asian noodles. This sauce will keep for up to two weeks in the fridge.

Makes 1½ cups

I TABLESPOON VEGETABLE OIL

2 GARLIC CLOVES, MINCED

¾ CUP CREAMY PEANUT BUTTER

¼ CUP LOW-SODIUM SOY SAUCE

2 TABLESPOONS RICE WINE VINEGAR

JUICE FROM I LEMON

I TABLESPOON HONEY

I TEASPOON FISH SAUCE

¼ TEASPOON CAYENNE PEPPER (OPTIONAL)

✦ Heat the vegetable oil in a small saucepan over medium heat. Add the garlic and toast in the oil, stirring frequently, until fragrant and beginning to turn golden brown, about 1 minute. Add the peanut butter, soy sauce, rice wine vinegar, lemon juice, honey, fish sauce, and cayenne (if using). Whisk together until a smooth consistency is achieved. Add a few tablespoons of water, if necessary, to thin the sauce. Cool in the refrigerator for 20 minutes before serving.

MANGO RAISIN CHUTNEY

Chutney adds a ton of flavor to many different dishes. At the Shop we serve this with the Jerk Chicken Balls (page 30) because it's the perfect counterpoint to the salty-spicy meatballs. Also, definitely try mixing this staple condiment into cooked rice or serve it alongside grilled chicken or fish. Alternatively, spread it on sandwiches, or stir it into a bit of mayo or yogurt for a quick dip. This sauce will keep for up to two weeks in the fridge.

Makes 3 cups

2 TABLESPOONS OLIVE OIL

I RED ONION, FINELY DICED

2 RIPE MANGOES, PEELED, PITTED, AND CHOPPED

I MEDIUM YUKON GOLD POTATO,
CUT INTO ¼-INCH DICE

½ CUP SUGAR

¼ TEASPOON CRUSHED RED PEPPER FLAKES

2 TABLESPOONS SWEET PAPRIKA

2 TEASPOONS SALT

½ CUP DARK RAISINS

½ CUP CHOPPED FRESH CILANTRO
(INCLUDING STEMS)

✤ Heat the olive oil in a medium saucepan. Add the onions and cook, stirring, until soft and translucent, about 10 minutes.

✤ Add the mangoes, potatoes, sugar, red pepper flakes, paprika, and salt. Heat the mixture, over medium-high heat, stirring frequently, until it begins to bubble. Reduce the heat to low and simmer until the potatoes are tender but not falling apart, about 15 minutes, continuing to stir frequently so that the chutney does not stick to the pan. Stir in the raisins and cilantro and allow to cool before serving.

CILANTRO YOGURT SAUCE

This sauce is the cool for our rich-and-spicy Tandoori Lamb Balls (page 40), but we also think it's pretty stellar when served alongside The Greek (page 10) and Mediterranean Lamb Balls (page 24). Try using this sauce as a marinade on pork, chicken, or lamb at your next barbecue. The acid and enzymes work like magic—you won't believe how tender your meat will turn. This sauce will keep for up to four days in the fridge.

Makes 3 cups

2 CUPS WHOLE-MILK YOGURT

½ RED ONION, FINELY DICED

I CUP CHOPPED FRESH CILANTRO

2 TABLESPOONS RED WINE VINEGAR

2 TEASPOONS SALT OR MORE TO TASTE

✤ Place the yogurt, onions, cilantro, vinegar, and salt in a medium bowl and whisk thoroughly until completely combined. Taste and adjust the seasoning, if desired.

THE SAUCES

BLUE CHEESE DRESSING

This rich dressing spikes through the creamy goodness and answers that "why doesn't my dressing ever taste this good?" question. This recipe works as well with Mini Buffalo Chicken Balls (page 9) as it does ladled over a thick wedge of iceberg lettuce topped with a few olives, carrot shavings, and crumbled bacon to create a more-than-satisfying classic salad. This dressing will keep for up to five days in the fridge.

Makes 2 cups

¾ CUP SOUR CREAM

⅓ CUP CRUMBLED BLUE CHEESE

⅓ CUP WHOLE MILK

⅓ CUP MAYONNAISE

I TEASPOON SALT OR MORE TO TASTE

I TABLESPOON RED WINE VINEGAR

✤ Place the sour cream, blue chese, milk, mayonnaise, salt, and vinegar in a medium bowl and whisk thoroughly until completely combined. Taste and adjust the seasoning, if desired.

THE SAUCES

THOUSAND ISLAND DRESSING

Sure, you want this as a quick and simple sauce for the Reuben Balls (page 29), but it is also great as a dipping sauce for shrimp, tortilla chips, or veggies. Don't skip the caraway seeds. Their distinctive aroma elevates this above and beyond store-bought dressing. This dressing will keep for up to a week in the fridge.

Makes 2 cups

2 TEASPOONS CARAWAY SEEDS

I CUP MAYONNAISE

⅓ CUP KETCHUP

⅓ CUP CHOPPED SWEET GHERKIN PICKLE

⅓ CUP WHOLE MILK

2 TEASPOONS SALT OR MORE TO TASTE

✦ Preheat the oven to 300° F.

✦ Place the caraway seeds on a rimmed baking sheet and toast for 4 minutes, until fragrant.

✦ Place the mayonnaise, ketchup, pickles, milk, salt, and caraway seeds in a medium bowl and whisk thoroughly until completely combined. Taste and adjust the seasoning, if desired.

THE SAUCES

CHAPTER 3

STICK TO YOUR BONES SIDES

"WE'VE GOT MORE THAN BALLS HANGING OUT
IN THE KITCHEN."

SEASONAL RISOTTO

We change up our risotto at least once a week at the Shop, so we have sixty or seventy rotating variations that reflect each season. Here are five of our favorites, one from each season, along with a classic basic recipe and a Venetian saffron variation. When making risotto, remember that the key is to stir the rice vigorously for the first half of the cooking process to create the creamy texture that is essential to the dish. Once the rice kernels become soft, stir more gently so as not to break them up.

BASIC RISOTTO

Serve with Classic Beef Meatballs (page 4)

Serves 4 to 6

4½ CUPS CHICKEN STOCK

2 TABLESPOONS OLIVE OIL

½ ONION, FINELY CHOPPED

2 CUPS ARBORIO RICE

½ CUP DRY WHITE WINE

I TEASPOON SALT OR MORE TO TASTE

2 TABLESPOONS UNSALTED BUTTER

½ CUP GRATED PARMESAN CHEESE

FRESHLY GROUND BLACK PEPPER

✤ Bring the chicken stock to a boil in a medium pot over medium-high heat and lower the flame to a simmer.

✤ Heat the olive oil in a large pot over medium heat. Add the onions and cook, stirring frequently, until they are soft and translucent, about 5 minutes.

✤ Add the rice and continue to cook, stirring constantly, for 4 minutes. Add the white wine and salt and continue to cook, stirring vigorously, until the wine has completely evaporated. Add 1 cup of the chicken stock and continue to cook and stir vigorously. When the chicken stock has been almost completely absorbed, about 7 minutes, add another cup of the chicken stock and continue to cook, stirring constantly but not vigorously. When the chicken stock has been almost completely absorbed, add the remaining 2½ cups chicken stock and continue to cook, for a total cooking time of about 25 minutes, stirring gently so that the rice does not stick.

✤ Stir in the butter and Parmesan and mix to incorporate. Taste and adjust the seasoning. Transfer to a platter or serving plates and finish with a generous turn of the pepper mill.

SPRING: PEA, CARROT, AND CHIVE RISOTTO

Serve with Bolognese Balls (page 6).

2 CUPS FRESH OR FROZEN PEAS

3 CARROTS, FINELY DICED

½ CUP CHOPPED FRESH CHIVES

✤ Bring a medium pot of salted water to a rolling boil over high heat. Add the peas and carrots and boil for 2 minutes (if using frozen peas, then just cook the carrots). Strain the vegetables through a fine-mesh sieve and cool under cold running water. Set aside.

✤ Add the cooked peas and carrots and the chives to the risotto when you add the butter and Parmesan.

SUMMER: FAVA BEAN, SPINACH, AND MUSHROOM RISOTTO

Serve with Veggie Balls (page 16).

1 CUP FRESH FAVA BEANS

ONE 9-OUNCE BAG BABY SPINACH LEAVES, ROUGHLY CHOPPED

2 TABLESPOONS OLIVE OIL

12 OUNCES WILD OR WHITE BUTTON MUSHROOMS, WIPED CLEAN AND ROUGHLY CHOPPED

PINCH OF SALT

✤ To shuck the fava beans, bring a medium pot of salted water to a rolling boil over high heat. Meanwhile, fill a small bowl with ice water.

✤ When the water is boiling, add the fava beans and cook for 90 seconds. Immediately remove the beans with a strainer and place them in the cold water until cool, about 2 minutes. Keep the pan of water at a boil. Drain the beans, then peel off the tough outer skins; set aside. Add the spinach to the boiling water, and cook for 1 minute. Strain the spinach and beans and cool under cold running water. Set aside.

✤ Heat the olive oil in a medium sauté pan over high heat. Add the mushrooms and salt and cook, stirring frequently, until the mushrooms begin to brown. Remove them from the heat and set aside.

✤ Add the cooked beans, spinach, and mushrooms to the risotto when you add the butter and Parmesan.

FALL: FENNEL RISOTTO

Serve with Mediterranean Lamb Balls (page 24).

FRONDS (GREEN LEAFY TOPS) FROM 2 FENNEL
BULBS, FINELY DICED (ABOUT I CUP)

I ONION, FINELY DICED

I TABLESPOON GROUND TOASTED FENNEL SEED

✤ Instead of adding the 2 tablespoons butter from the Basic Risotto recipe at the end, melt them at the beginning of cooking in a large sauté pan over medium heat. Then, add the fresh fennel, onions, and ground fennel and cook, stirring frequently, until the fresh fennel is soft and the onions are soft and translucent, about 10 minutes. Add a few tablespoons of water, if necessary, to ensure that the vegetables do not brown. Set aside and proceed with the recipe as directed

✤ Add the cooked fennel mixture to the risotto when you add the Parmesan at the end.

WINTER: PROSCIUTTO RISOTTO

Serve with Chicken Meatballs (page 12).

½ POUND PROSCIUTTO, FINELY CHOPPED

✤ Add the prosciutto along with the onions at the beginning of the cooking process.

VARIATION: SAFFRON RISOTTO

We couldn't not include this seasonless classic. Buy the best-quality saffron threads you can find.
The saffron pairs perfectly with Bouillabaisse Balls (page 23).

I TEASPOON SAFFRON THREADS

¼ CUP WARM WATER

✤ Soak the saffron threads in the warm water for 5 minutes. Set aside. Add the saffron to the risotto along with the final addition of chicken stock. Proceed with the recipe as directed.

CREAMY POLENTA

When it comes to polenta, freshly milled corn makes all the difference. We are lucky enough to have Wild Hive Farm in Clinton Corners, New York, grind the polenta for the Shop (you can order it at www.wildhivefarm .com). Bob's Red Mill is a great alternative that can be found in many supermarkets, health food stores, and online (www.bobsredmill.com). This recipe requires a slight investment of time, but the result is mind-blowingly good. Just make sure to whisk the mixture constantly until the polenta comes to a boil; otherwise it can easily burn. Polenta is incredible served alongside just about any kind of meatball, but it is classically served as a stand-alone dish. Try it with a ladleful of Classic Tomato Sauce (page 56) or Spicy Meat Sauce (page 57) on top.

Serves 4 to 6

1 TEASPOON SALT

2 CUPS COARSELY GROUND CORNMEAL OR GRITS (NOT INSTANT POLENTA)

½ CUP HEAVY CREAM

⅓ CUP GRATED PARMESAN CHEESE

4 TABLESPOONS (½ STICK) UNSALTED BUTTER

❖ Bring 9 cups water and the salt to a rolling boil in a medium pot over high heat. Whisk in the cornmeal and continue whisking until the water begins to boil again. Lower the heat to the lowest setting and continue to cook, stirring every 5 minutes, for 1 hour.

❖ Remove from the heat and whisk in the cream, Parmesan, and butter. Allow to sit for 10 minutes before serving.

MASHED POTATOES

When it comes to mashed potatoes, there is only one rule: Use more butter, cream, and salt than you think you need. The sweet flavor and creamy, moist texture of Yukon golds make them the perfect potatoes to mash. If you're making mashed potatoes in advance, add a little extra milk to thin the consistency for reheating. Because Yukon golds have a thin, tender skin, we choose to skip the peeling and go straight to the eating. Honestly, we can eat bowls of these mashed potatoes on their own, but they pair well with pretty much any meatball.

Serves 4 to 6

5 LARGE YUKON GOLD POTATOES, QUARTERED

½ CUP HEAVY CREAM

¼ CUP WHOLE MILK

3 TABLESPOONS UNSALTED BUTTER

2 TEASPOONS SALT

✤ Place the potatoes in a large pot with enough water to cover by 2 inches. Bring to a boil over high heat, then reduce the heat to low and simmer until fork-tender, about 25 minutes. Drain thoroughly, until completely dry.

✤ Place the potatoes in a bowl, and while they are still hot, add the cream, milk, butter, and salt. Mash with a wire whisk or potato masher until well combined and relatively smooth. Serve immediately.

STICK TO YOUR BONES SIDES

SMASHED TURNIPS WITH FRESH HORSERADISH

We love turnips and don't want you to pass them by the next time you're at the market. When cooked right, their earthy flavor is seriously irresistible. At the Shop people go crazy for them. The kick from the horseradish brings out the natural sweetness, and the sour cream adds a tangy, rich element. We love these with the Salmon Balls (page 34) or Venison, aka Bambi, Balls (page 42).

Serves 4 to 6

8 LARGE TURNIPS (ABOUT 2 POUNDS), PEELED AND QUARTERED

½ CUP SOUR CREAM

6 SCALLIONS, THINLY SLICED

2 TABLESPOONS FRESHLY GRATED HORSERADISH OR MORE TO TASTE

2 TEASPOONS SALT

✤ Place the turnips in a large pot with enough water to cover by 2 inches. Bring to a boil over high heat, then reduce the heat to low and simmer until fork-tender, about 25 minutes. Drain thoroughly, until completely dry.

✤ Place the turnips in a bowl and, while they are still hot, add the sour cream, scallions, horseradish, and salt. Mash with a wire whisk or potato masher until well combined but still chunky. Serve immediately.

STICK TO YOUR BONES SIDES

CANDIED YAMS

We serve this comforting and nostalgic Thanksgiving favorite throughout the fall and winter months. Yams are sweet on their own, so you don't want to overdo it with the marshmallows. Here we provide just enough to give you a sweet taste every few bites. Candied yams are a natural for the Gobble, Gobble Balls (page 39), of course, but try them with the Spicy Pork Meatballs (page 21) too.

Serves 4 to 6

2 POUNDS YAMS, PEELED AND CUT INTO
2-INCH PIECES

5 TABLESPOONS UNSALTED BUTTER

¼ CUP HEAVY CREAM

¼ CUP WHOLE MILK

2 TEASPOONS SALT

¼ TEASPOON GROUND CINNAMON

¼ TEASPOON GROUND ALLSPICE

½ TEASPOON FRESHLY GROUND BLACK PEPPER

1 CUP MINI MARSHMALLOWS

✤ Preheat the oven to 400°F.

✤ Place the yams in a medium pot with enough water to cover by 2 inches. Bring to a boil over high heat, then reduce the heat to low and simmer until fork-tender, about 20 minutes. Drain thoroughly, until completely dry.

✤ Place the yams in a large bowl and add the butter, cream, milk, salt, cinnamon, allspice, and pepper. Mash with a wire whisk or potato masher until well combined. Taste and adjust the seasoning.

✤ Spread the mashed yams into the bottom of a 9-inch square baking dish. Dot with the marshmallows, pushing them into the yams so that they are sticking out halfway.

✤ Bake until the marshmallows are melted and golden brown, about 20 minutes. Serve immediately.

PROVOLONE AND WILD MUSHROOM BISCUITS

Using tangy provolone is a nice departure from the usual cheddar in these light biscuits, which we created with the leftover bits of cheese that we serve on our sandwiches. When we put these on the menu, they sell out in two hours. Slice them in half and load them with your favorite ball. We like to make these really big, but you can use a smaller biscuit cutter. Just check the biscuits for doneness a minute sooner. If wild mushrooms aren't available, use portobellos or buttons.

Makes six 4-inch biscuits

2 TABLESPOONS OLIVE OIL

6 OUNCES FRESH WILD MUSHROOMS, SUCH AS BLACK TRUMPETS, CHANTERELLES, MORELS, OR PORCINI, WIPED CLEAN AND CUT INTO ½-INCH PIECES

PINCH PLUS ¼ TEASPOON SALT

2¼ CUPS ALL-PURPOSE FLOUR

1¼ TABLESPOONS BAKING POWDER

8 TABLESPOONS (1 STICK) COLD UNSALTED BUTTER, CUBED

¾ CUP WHOLE MILK, CHILLED

½ POUND PROVOLONE CHEESE, GRATED

3 SCALLIONS, THINLY SLICED

1 LARGE EGG YOLK WHISKED WITH 2 TABLESPOONS WATER (TO BRUSH ON BISCUIT TOPS)

✤ Preheat the oven to 400°F.

✤ Heat the olive oil in a medium frying pan over high heat. Add the mushrooms and a pinch of salt and sauté, stirring frequently, until they are browned and all of their liquid has evaporated, 4 to 5 minutes. Transfer to a bowl and let cool in the refrigerator.

✤ Combine the flour, baking powder, and the remaining ¼ teaspoon salt in the bowl of a food processor. Add the butter cubes and pulse 5 to 8 times, until the butter is just incorporated and the mixture resembles little peas.

✤ Transfer the dough to a bowl and, using a wooden spoon, mix in the milk and two-thirds of the provolone, the cooled mushrooms, and the scallions until just incorporated.

✤ Divide the dough into 6 equal portions and form each into a loosely packed ball. Place on a rimmed baking sheet, leaving 1 inch between each biscuit.

✤ Brush each biscuit with the egg wash and sprinkle the remaining provolone over the tops. Bake for 20 to 22 minutes, rotating the pan halfway through. Serve warm or at room temperature.

WHITE BEANS

he upside to these beans is that they are totally delicious. The downside is that they take a seriously long time to soak and cook (plan on starting these the night before you intend to serve them). But please don't take any shortcuts, or you may end up with undercooked beans, which are not so delicious. For the perfect combination, try Classic Beef Meatballs (page 4) with Classic Tomato Sauce (page 56) over a heap of these beans. They are also a great addition to a salad, and can turn simple greens into a protein-rich meal.

Serves 4 to 6

2 CUPS SMALL WHITE BEANS

½ SMALL ONION

I SMALL CARROT, CUT IN HALF CROSSWISE

I CELERY STALK, QUARTERED CROSSWISE

2 GARLIC CLOVES

I BAY LEAF

¼ CUP OLIVE OIL

2 TABLESPOONS SALT

✤ Soak the beans overnight in a pot with at least six times their volume of water.

✤ Transfer the beans along with the soaking liquid to a large pot. Add enough water to the liquid to cover by 4 inches. Add the onions, carrot, celery, garlic, and bay leaf and bring to a boil over high heat. Reduce the heat to low and simmer, stirring occasionally, until the beans are tender, about 1½ hours.

✤ Drain the beans, discard the bay leaf, and transfer the beans to a large mixing bowl. Remove the onion, carrot, celery, and garlic and finely chop. Return the vegetables and garlic to the bowl. Add the olive oil and salt and mix gently but thoroughly before serving.

CHAPTER

4

THE
VEG

"WE GIVE OUR VEGETABLES FULL-ON PROPS. BRAISED,
GRILLED, ROASTED, MARINATED, IT'S ALL GOOD."

HONEY-ROASTED CARROTS WITH PRUNES, WALNUTS, AND MINT

Carrots are often underappreciated, and we think they are one of those incredible vegetables that is worth another look. We were inspired to re-create a modern version of a classic Jewish dish called tzimmis, which is served to welcome in the new year. With its great balance of savory carrots, refreshing mint, and lemon juice, plus crunchy, earthy walnuts and sweet honey and prunes, this is one of our go-to roasted veg dishes at the Shop. Serve warm or at room temperature.

Serves 4 to 6

FOR THE CARROTS

8 LARGE CARROTS CUT INTO 3 X I-INCH PIECES
(LIKE THICK-CUT FRENCH FRIES)

¼ CUP OLIVE OIL

I TEASPOON SALT

½ CUP HONEY

FOR THE TOPPING

¼ CUP CHOPPED PITTED PRUNES

I TABLESPOON OLIVE OIL

¼ CUP CHOPPED FRESH MINT

¼ CUP CHOPPED TOASTED WALNUTS

½ TEASPOON SALT

SQUEEZE OF FRESH LEMON JUICE

✢ Preheat the oven to 450°F.

✢ Toss the carrots with the olive oil in a large bowl, and coat thoroughly. Add the salt and toss to coat.

✢ Combine the honey and ½ cup warm water in a small bowl and stir until thoroughly mixed.

✢ Lay the carrots out on a large rimmed baking sheet or roasting pan so that they are evenly spaced and do not touch one another. Drizzle with the honey mixture and put the carrots in the oven to roast.

✢ Roast until all of the water has evaporated and the carrots are soft and beginning to brown, 35 to 40 minutes.

✢ While the carrots are roasting, prepare the topping. Mix the prunes and olive oil in a small bowl. Work the mixture so that the prunes are thoroughly coated and not sticking together. Add mint, walnuts, salt, and lemon juice and mix thoroughly to combine.

✢ Remove the carrots from the oven and arrange them on a serving dish. Spoon the topping over the carrots and serve.

ROASTED BRUSSELS SPROUTS WITH APPLES AND HONEY-ROASTED PECANS

Brussels sprouts are one of the highlights of the fall market. If you're lucky you can buy them attached to the stalk. When roasted, the outer leaves become nicely browned, and in this recipe the flavor is intensified by the addition of apples and onions. The honey-roasted pecans add a wonderful sweet and salty crunch and are a bonus recipe here—you can snack on these with a cocktail too. And while we keep the veggies all vegetarian at the Shop, if you want to, roast a little bacon or pancetta along with them. The results will speak for themselves.

Serves 4 to 6

I POUND BRUSSELS SPROUTS, TRIMMED
AND HALVED

I LARGE ONION, CUT INTO I-INCH PIECES

¼ CUP OLIVE OIL

2 TEASPOONS SALT OR TO TASTE

2 BAKING APPLES, SUCH AS BRAEBURN OR
GRANNY SMITH, PEELED, CORED, AND
CUT INTO I-INCH PIECES

¼ CUP APPLE CIDER VINEGAR

I CUP HONEY-ROASTED PECANS (RECIPE FOLLOWS)

FRESHLY GROUND BLACK PEPPER

✤ Preheat the oven to 500°F.

✤ Place the Brussels sprouts and onions in a 9 × 13-inch baking dish. Add the olive oil and salt, and toss to coat.

✤ Roast until the Brussels sprouts begin to brown, about 15 minutes. Add the apples, mix, and return to the oven. Continue roasting, turning every 10 minutes, until the Brussels sprouts and onions are fully cooked and tender and the apples are beginning to soften, about 20 minutes.

✤ Remove the dish from the oven, add the vinegar, and toss to incorporate. Season with additional salt, if desired, and transfer to a platter. Top with the pecans and a generous sprinkle of pepper. Serve immediately.

HONEY-ROASTED PECANS

Make extra pecans and store them in a resealable container with a tight-fitting lid in the pantry or a cabinet. If they get a bit stale or soggy, you can always roast them again for a few minutes.

Makes 1 cup

I CUP PECAN HALVES
2 TABLESPOONS HONEY
I TEASPOON SALT

Preheat the oven to 325°F.

Place the pecans on a rimmed baking sheet. Drizzle on the honey, add the salt, and toss to coat.

Roast, tossing every 5 minutes, until the pecans are deep brown, well roasted, and let off a strong, nutty aroma, about 20 minutes.

Remove the pecans from the oven and allow to cool before using or serving.

ROASTED FENNEL WITH RAISINS, WALNUTS, AND PARSLEY

Fennel is a staple ingredient at the Shop. It's extremely versatile and just as delicious thinly sliced into a salad as it is roasted as an accompaniment. Don't discard the green fronds; they are very flavorful, and you can use them for the Fennel Risotto (page 77).

Serves 4 to 6

4 FENNEL HEADS

4 TABLESPOONS OLIVE OIL

2 TEASPOONS SALT

¼ CUP WALNUTS, TOASTED AND FINELY CHOPPED

¼ CUP ROUGHLY CHOPPED RAISINS

¼ CUP CHOPPED FRESH PARSLEY

JUICE FROM I LEMON

✧ Preheat the oven to 450°F.

✧ Slice the fennel into ½-inch-thick wedges, making sure to leave the bolster intact so that the fennel pieces stay together. Place the wedges in a 9 × 13-inch baking dish. Drizzle with 2 tablespoons of the olive oil and 1 teaspoon of the salt. Add 1 cup water.

✧ Roast until the fennel is soft and fully cooked through, the edges are slightly brown, and the water is completely evaporated, about 40 minutes.

✧ While the fennel is roasting, combine the walnuts, raisins, parsley, the remaining 2 tablespoons olive oil and 1 teaspoon salt, and a squeeze of lemon juice in a small bowl and mix well. Make sure that the raisins are well coated with olive oil and not clumped together.

✧ Remove the fennel from the oven and arrange on a large serving platter. Top with the raisin mixture and serve.

BRAISED COLLARD GREENS

Collard greens are sweet and yummy, but you need to cook them all the way through or they can be bitter and tough. Cooking them in salted water will speed up the process so you can get these greens into your mouth as soon as possible. A little splash of vinegar at the end of cooking helps brighten the flavor. We use these as a bed for the Bolognese Balls (page 6), but they work well with pretty much any meatball in the book.

Serves 4 to 6

THE VEG

2 BUNCHES COLLARD GREENS, WELL RINSED

3 TABLESPOONS OLIVE OIL

4 GARLIC CLOVES, MINCED

2 TEASPOONS SALT

¼ CUP RED WINE VINEGAR

✤ Bring a large pot of salted water to a boil over high heat.

✤ Cut the tough stem ends from the collards and discard. Cut the leaves and tender stems into large bite-size pieces. Submerge the collards in the boiling water and cook, stirring once or twice, for 6 minutes. Drain the water and set the collards aside.

✤ Heat the olive oil in a large pot over medium heat and add the garlic and salt. Cook, stirring frequently, until the garlic is just beginning to brown, 1 to 2 minutes. Add the collards, vinegar, and ¼ cup water to the pot and continue to cook, stirring constantly, until the collards are soft and all of the water has evaporated, about 10 minutes. If the water evaporates too quickly, add a few extra tablespoons so that the collards have time to cook fully; they should be very tender. Serve immediately.

BRAISED KALE WITH
ANCHOVIES AND GARLIC

Green leafy vegetables like kale are extremely healthy, and kale is one of our favorites. The key to this recipe is cooking the anchovies and garlic until they are falling apart, almost melting into the dish. If you have an aversion to anchovies, feel free to leave them out. Just add a pinch more salt. Serve alongside Mediterranean Lamb Balls (page 24).

Serves 4 to 6

2 BUNCHES KALE, TOUGH STEMS REMOVED,
LEAVES AND TENDER STEMS CUT INTO
BITE-SIZE PIECES

2 TABLESPOONS OLIVE OIL

4 GARLIC CLOVES, MINCED

4 ANCHOVY FILLETS PACKED IN OIL

2 TEASPOONS SALT

¼ TEASPOON CRUSHED RED PEPPER FLAKES

¼ CUP TOMATO PASTE

✤ Bring a large pot of salted water to a boil. Submerge the kale in the boiling water and cook, stirring once or twice, for 4 minutes. Drain and set aside.

✤ Heat the olive oil in a large pot over very low heat. Add the garlic, anchovies, salt, and red pepper flakes. Cook, stirring frequently, until the anchovies have disintegrated and the garlic is just beginning to brown, about 10 minutes. Add the tomato paste and continue cooking, stirring constantly, until the tomato paste has turned a deep, brick-red color, about 10 minutes.

✤ Add the kale and ¼ cup water to the pot and continue to cook, stirring constantly, until the kale and the tomato mixture have fully combined, all of the water has evaporated, and the kale is fully tender, about 10 minutes. If the water evaporates too quickly, add a few extra tablespoons so that the kale has time to cook fully. Serve immediately.

THE VEG

ROASTED BEETS WITH WATERCRESS, ALMONDS, AND PECORINO

Beets are so sweet and delicious that at the restaurant we try to feature them as often as possible. We also try to make things a little bit more interesting by adding pecorino to the beets instead of traditional goat cheese. FYI, the longer the beets are marinated, the better they tend to taste, so plan to prepare this dish in advance.

Serves 4 to 6

4 LARGE RED BEETS OR 8 SMALL
(ABOUT 1½ POUNDS TOTAL), TRIMMED

1 BUNCH WATERCRESS, ENDS TRIMMED AND
DISCARDED, CUT INTO 1-INCH-LONG PIECES

¼ CUP OLIVE OIL

1 TEASPOON SALT

1 LEMON

¼ CUP ALMONDS, TOASTED AND ROUGHLY
CHOPPED

¼ CUP GRATED AGED PECORINO CHEESE

FRESHLY GROUND BLACK PEPPER

✦ Preheat the oven to 400°F.

✦ Place the beets in a 9 × 13-inch baking dish. Fill the dish halfway with water and cover it with aluminum foil.

✦ Roast until the beets are fully cooked (a paring knife should pass into the center of the largest beet with no resistance), about 1 hour.

✦ Remove the beets from the oven and allow to cool for 15 minutes. Using a paper towel, rub the skin from the outside of the beets. Slice the beets into bite-size hunks or wedges and transfer to a bowl to cool to room temperature. Add the watercress, olive oil, salt, and a squeeze of lemon juice and toss to combine.

✦ Arrange the beet mixture on a serving platter and sprinkle with the almonds and pecorino. Finish with a few grinds of pepper. Let sit for at least one hour or more to marinate. Serve at room temperature.

MUSIC, MUSIC, MUSIC. We can't stress enough how important music is to your dining experience, no matter where you eat. Whether at the Shop or at home, we always have something great cranking from our speakers. The music we play tends to reflect whatever mood we're in. Music can evoke memories, transport you to a different place and time, help create a romantic setting, or boost a celebration. At the Shop, you will hear everything from Billie Holiday to Biggie Smalls, from The Rolling Stones to The Del Vikings. Our collection of music is vast. We base our playlist on the time of day or night, and what sort of guests are dining with us. We play our music loud when the place is really buzzing, from say 9:00 p.m. on, and

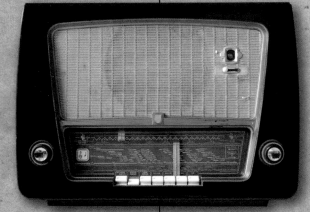

then we crank it up even more after midnight. We love it when a great song comes on and the crowd gets involved rocking out and singing along.

So when you're planning your next get-together be sure to consider your music menu in addition to your food menu. Have you invited a sophisticated couple or is it more of a raucous bunch? Will kids be there? How about the in-laws (now is the perfect time to throw on some oldies or a little Frank Sinatra and watch what may be an uncomfortable situation transform into smiles and laughter!)?

We promise, listening to Led Zeppelin or De La Soul over a bowl of meatballs is nothing short of amazing. Don't be afraid to push PLAY while cooking either—music is the greatest motivator.

ROASTED CAULIFLOWER
WITH HOT CHERRY PEPPERS
AND BREAD CRUMBS

If prepared with a bit of inspiration, cauliflower can taste complex and flavorful. As with all recipes, the simpler the preparation, the more important attention to detail becomes, and with this dish, it's all about the high-heat roasting. Don't be afraid of a few burned edges. Cauliflower is low in sugar, so roast it hot and fast so that it browns well but keeps some of its wonderful crunchy texture. Make sure you don't overcrowd the roasting pan, as this will cause the vegetable to steam instead of roast. You'll love this alongside our Bouillabaisse Balls (page 23).

Serves 4 to 6

I LARGE HEAD CAULIFLOWER, CORED AND
CUT INTO LARGE FLORETS

2 TABLESPOONS OLIVE OIL

2 TEASPOONS SALT

½ CUP FINELY SLICED HOT CHERRY PEPPERS
(STEMS AND SEEDS REMOVED)

2 TABLESPOONS PICKLING JUICE FROM
THE HOT CHERRY PEPPERS

2 TABLESPOONS CHOPPED FRESH
PARSLEY

SALT

½ CUP CRUSHED GARLIC CROUTONS (PAGE 119)
OR STORE-BOUGHT CROUTONS

✤ Preheat the oven to 500°F.

✤ Place the cauliflower florets in a 9 × 13-inch baking dish. Add the olive oil and salt and toss, making sure the cauliflower is well coated.

✤ Roast until the edges of the cauliflower begin to brown, about 15 minutes. Toss the cauliflower and continue to roast, tossing every 5 minutes, until tender but firm and well browned all over, about 10 minutes.

✤ Remove the cauliflower from the oven and transfer to a large mixing bowl. Add the cherry peppers, pepper juice, and parsley and toss to thoroughly combine. Add salt to taste.

✤ Transfer the cauliflower to a serving dish and sprinkle with the crushed croutons just before serving to ensure that they stay crispy.

ROASTED BUTTERNUT SQUASH WITH SABA AND RICOTTA SALATA

Saba (*mosto cotto*), a reduction of grape must, has a flavor similar to that of balsamic vinegar. It is a largely undiscovered treasure here in the States, but is commonly found in Italian pantries. Our ace recipe tester, Alison Ladman, came up with an easy recipe for a homemade version. You can also use aged balsamic vinegar that's been reduced by half its volume. If no specialty grapes, such as Concord, are available, a mixture of red and white grapes works well too. A drizzle of this syrup brings out the sweetness of the roasted squash and beautifully offsets the saltiness of the drier ricotta salata cheese.

Serves 4 to 6

2 MEDIUM BUTTERNUT SQUASH, PEELED, SEEDED, AND CUT INTO I-INCH CHUNKS

¼ CUP OLIVE OIL

I TEASPOON SALT

3 TABLESPOONS SABA (RECIPE FOLLOWS)

¼ POUND RICOTTA SALATA CHEESE

¼ CUP WALNUTS, TOASTED AND FINELY CHOPPED

✢ Preheat the oven to 450°F.

✢ Place the squash on a rimmed baking sheet and toss with the olive oil and salt. Arrange the squash so that none of the pieces are touching.

✢ Roast until the squash is soft and golden brown around the edges, about 45 minutes.

✢ Remove the squash from the oven and transfer to a serving platter. Drizzle with the saba, crumble the ricotta salata over the squash, and sprinkle with the walnuts. Serve immediately.

~ SABA ~

Makes about ½ cup

2 POUNDS WINE GRAPES, SUCH AS CONCORD OR CHAMPAGNE

I FRESH ROSEMARY SPRIG

Place the grapes in a large pot and crush with a potato masher so that they release their juices. Add the rosemary and bring to a boil over medium heat (leave the seeds and stems in the pot). Cook the mixture, stirring and crushing frequently, until the grapes have completely broken down and lost their juices, about 15 minutes. Strain the contents through a fine-mesh sieve into a small pot. Make sure to squeeze all of the juice from the grapes (pressing with the back of a wooden spoon works well). Discard the seeds, stems, and rosemary.

Bring the juices back to a boil over medium heat and slowly reduce until a syrupy consistency is reached (the liquid will coat the back of a metal spoon lightly), about 40 minutes. It is very easy to scorch the syrup, so test it frequently by drizzling it on a plate. If it has reduced too much, add a little water to reconstitute. The syrup will thicken significantly when it is cool.

PARSNIPS WITH CHILES, CORIANDER, AND WATERCRESS

People can be, well, persnickety, about parsnips. We think they are the unsung heroes of the veggie bin: We know them to be sweet like carrots but also have a wonderful, earthy flavor. The ground coriander used here adds an evocative fragrance, and brown sugar helps to enhance the parsnips' natural sweetness.

Serves 4 to 6

6 PARSNIPS, PEELED AND CUT INTO 3 X 1-INCH PIECES (LIKE THICK-CUT FRENCH FRIES)

2 TEASPOONS GROUND CORIANDER

1 TEASPOON CRUSHED RED PEPPER FLAKES

1 TEASPOON SALT

2 TABLESPOONS DARK BROWN SUGAR

4 TABLESPOONS OLIVE OIL

½ BUNCH WATERCRESS, ¼ INCH OF TOUGH STEMS CUT OFF, AND REMAINING WATERCRESS TORN INTO 2-INCH PIECES

JUICE FROM ½ LEMON

¼ CUP ALMONDS, TOASTED AND FINELY CHOPPED

✤ Preheat the oven to 400°F.

✤ Toss the parsnips with the coriander, red pepper flakes, salt, brown sugar, and 2 tablespoons of the olive oil in a large bowl. Place the seasoned parsnips in a 9 × 13-inch baking dish.

✤ Roast until the parsnips are soft and beginning to brown, tossing once to ensure even browning, about 40 minutes.

✤ Remove the parsnips from the oven and allow to cool to room temperature.

✤ Transfer the parsnips to a medium bowl and add the watercress, the remaining 2 tablespoons olive oil, and the lemon juice and toss until well coated. Transfer to a serving platter and top with almonds before serving.

CREAMED SPINACH

Creamed spinach is something we crave. Everyone else seems to love it too, because it's soulfully satisfying. Another great thing about creamed spinach is that its high fat content allows it to freeze extremely well. Go ahead and make a double batch (and see if the other half actually makes it into the freezer). Swiss chard works just as well as spinach in this recipe. While this side is incredible on its own, wait until you try it with Chicken Meatballs (page 12).

Serves 4 to 6

TWO 12-OUNCE BAGS BABY SPINACH LEAVES

1½ CUPS PARMESAN CREAM SAUCE (PAGE 60)

¼ CUP BREAD CRUMBS

¼ CUP GRATED PARMESAN CHEESE

FRESHLY GROUND BLACK PEPPER

✤ Preheat the oven to 425°F. Fill a large bowl halfway with water and ice. Set aside.

✤ Bring a large pot of salted water to a boil over high heat. Add the spinach and cook for 30 seconds, stirring once or twice. Drain the spinach and plunge it into the bowl with the ice water. Stir to cool. Drain the spinach again, squeezing out any excess water.

✤ Mix the spinach and Parmesan cream sauce in a large bowl. Spoon the mixture into 6 small ovenproof casseroles and top with the bread crumbs, Parmesan, and a healthy grating of pepper.

✤ Bake until bubbling and browned on top, about 35 minutes. Remove from the oven and serve warm.

THE VEG

BRAISED GREEN BEANS

While we love the snap of quickly blanched green beans, we also love this preparation, which leaves the green beans almost meltingly tender. They're ready when they are completely soft and cooked through, and all the delicious seasonings have been absorbed by the beans. They are perfect alongside grilled or baked fish, or with our Veal Meatballs (page 48).

Serves 4 to 6

2 POUNDS GREEN BEANS, TRIMMED

2 TABLESPOONS OLIVE OIL

4 GARLIC CLOVES, MINCED

½ TEASPOON CRUSHED RED PEPPER FLAKES

2 TEASPOONS SALT OR TO TASTE

¼ CUP TOMATO PASTE

✤ Bring a large pot of salted water to a boil. Submerge the beans in the boiling water and cook, stirring once or twice, for 4 minutes. Drain and set the beans aside.

✤ Heat the olive oil in a large pot over medium heat. Add the garlic, red pepper flakes, and salt and cook, stirring frequently, until the garlic is just beginning to brown, 1 to 2 minutes. Add the tomato paste and continue cooking, stirring constantly, until the tomato paste has turned a deep, brick-red color, about 10 minutes.

✤ Add the green beans and ¼ cup water to the pot and continue to cook, stirring constantly, until the beans and tomato paste have mixed completely and all of the water has evaporated, about 10 minutes. If the water evaporates too quickly, add a few extra tablespoons so that the beans have time to cook fully; they should be very tender. Taste and adjust the seasoning. Serve immediately.

MARINATED MUSHROOMS

Marinated button mushrooms are typically included in an antipasto platter, but they make a great solo starter too. Use your favorite combination of wild or domestic mushrooms and, for a heartier dish, try swapping the white wine for red. These mushrooms will last for up to a week in the refrigerator.

Serves 4 to 6

¼ CUP OLIVE OIL

TWO 12-OUNCE PACKAGES BUTTON MUSHROOMS,
RINSED AND PATTED DRY

2 GARLIC CLOVES, CRUSHED WITH THE SIDE
OF A CHEF'S KNIFE

2 TEASPOONS FRESH THYME

1 TABLESPOON SALT

¼ TEASPOON FRESHLY GROUND BLACK PEPPER

¼ CUP DRY WHITE WINE

½ CUP CHOPPED FRESH PARSLEY

JUICE FROM 1 LEMON

✤ Preheat the oven to 500°F.

✤ Heat the olive oil in a large ovenproof frying pan over high heat. Add the mushrooms, garlic, thyme, salt, and pepper and cook, stirring once or twice, until the mushrooms begin to brown, about 4 minutes.

✤ Place the skillet in the oven and cook for 10 minutes, stirring once after 5 minutes.

✤ Transfer the skillet to the stove top over high heat. Add the white wine and with a wooden spoon scrape up any bits that have clung to the pan. Allow the wine to come to a boil, then add the parsley and lemon juice.

✤ Transfer the mushrooms along with their cooking liquid to a container and allow to cool. Cover with a tight-fitting lid and place in the refrigerator until ready to serve.

BRAISED SWISS CHARD
WITH PESTO AND LEMON

While braising may be a favorite cold weather cooking technique, we often braise with spring and summer vegetables. We tend to prefer most braised greens fully cooked, so don't be afraid to overblanch these greens. The key to this dish is taking the time to cook the chard with the pesto so that the greens absorb all of the flavor. We like to pair this with Bunny Balls (page 50).

Serves 4 to 6

2 BUNCHES SWISS CHARD, TOUGH STEMS
REMOVED, LEAVES AND TENDER STEMS
CUT INTO BITE-SIZE PIECES

2 TABLESPOONS OLIVE OIL

I ONION, FINELY CHOPPED

I TEASPOON SALT

½ CUP SPINACH-BASIL PESTO (PAGE 58)

SQUEEZE OF FRESH LEMON JUICE

✤ Bring a large pot of salted water to a boil over high heat. Submerge the chard in the boiling water and cook, stirring once or twice, for 2 minutes. Drain and set the chard aside.

✤ Heat the olive oil in another large pot over medium-high heat. Add the onions and salt and cook, stirring frequently, until tender, about 10 minutes. Do not allow the onions to brown. Add a few tablespoons of water, if necessary.

✤ Add the chard and pesto to the pot and continue cooking, stirring constantly, until the chard and pesto have mixed completely and any remaining water has evaporated, about 5 minutes.

✤ Finish with a squeeze of lemon, stir, and serve immediately.

MARINATED PEPPERS AND POTATOES WITH OLIVES AND CAPERS

Marinated peppers paired with potatoes is another star addition to an antipasto platter, and is equally brilliant served alongside The Spaniard (page 14). This dish will hold for up to three days in the refrigerator and tends to taste better when the potatoes have time to absorb the marinade. If you do prepare it in advance, make sure you bring it up to room temperature before serving.

Serves 4 to 6

2 RED BELL PEPPERS, CORED, HALVED
AND SEEDED

2 YELLOW BELL PEPPERS, CORED, HALVED,
AND SEEDED

3 TEASPOONS OLIVE OIL

4 TEASPOONS SALT

3 LARGE YUKON GOLD POTATOES, UNPEELED,
CUT INTO 1½-INCH WEDGES

6 FRESH BASIL LEAVES, TORN INTO QUARTERS

¼ CUP PITTED KALAMATA OLIVES, QUARTERED

1 TABLESPOON SALTED CAPERS, SOAKED IN WARM
WATER FOR 10 MINUTES AND DRAINED

✤ Preheat the oven to 550°F or the highest setting.

✤ Place the bell peppers in a 9 × 13-inch roasting pan. Drizzle with 1 teaspoon of the olive oil and sprinkle with 1 teaspoon of the salt. Toss well to coat.

✤ Roast the peppers until the skins begin to blister and peel, about 25 minutes. Transfer the peppers to a bowl and cover tightly with plastic wrap so that no steam escapes. Set aside.

✤ Place the potatoes in a pot and cover with cold water. Add 2 teaspoons of the salt and bring to a boil. Reduce the heat to low and allow the potatoes to simmer until just tender when pierced with a fork, about 15 minutes. Drain thoroughly and set the potatoes aside to cool.

✤ Remove the peppers from the bowl and lay them skin side up on a cutting board. Scrape away the skin with a chef's knife and discard. Cut the peppers into 1-inch strips.

✤ Transfer the peppers and potatoes to a mixing bowl. Add the basil, olives, capers, and the remaining 1 teaspoon salt and 2 teaspoons olive oil and toss to combine. Serve at room temperature.

ASPARAGUS WITH WHOLE-GRAIN MUSTARD VINAIGRETTE

Asparagus stands up well to being roasted at high heat or on the grill. Extreme heat helps caramelize the veggie and bring out its sweetness. The asparagus is meant to be served al dente—please don't overcook it, as a little toothsome bite is welcome here. Make sure you use whole-grain mustard for its great texture.

Serves 4 to 6

¼ CUP OLIVE OIL

3 TABLESPOONS RED WINE VINEGAR

3 TABLESPOONS WHOLE-GRAIN MUSTARD

¼ CUP CHOPPED FRESH PARSLEY

I TEASPOON SALT

2 BUNCHES LARGE ASPARAGUS, TRIMMED

❖ Preheat the oven to 450°F.

❖ Whisk together the olive oil, vinegar, mustard, parsley, and salt in a small mixing bowl. Toss the asparagus with the mustard vinaigrette in a 9 × 13-inch baking dish.

❖ Roast until the asparagus is just tender, about 10 minutes.

❖ Arrange the asparagus on a large serving platter, being sure to scrape all of the burned bits of mustard from the bottom of the pan along with the asparagus. Serve immediately.

MARINATED GRILLED EGGPLANT

Another addictive antipasto dish—the smoky grilled flavor here is a bright note with the marinade. This is best served at room temperature, so plan on making it in advance. Eggplant is extremely absorbent—don't worry if it soaks up all of the olive oil. The oil provides plenty of flavor and helps prevent the eggplants from burning over the open flame.

Serves 6

2 LARGE EGGPLANTS, SLICED INTO
1-INCH-THICK ROUNDS

¼ CUP OLIVE OIL

1 TEASPOON SALT

¼ CUP CHOPPED FRESH PARSLEY

¼ CUP CAPERS, RINSED, DRAINED, AND CHOPPED

1 GARLIC CLOVE, MINCED

2 TABLESPOONS RED WINE VINEGAR

SQUEEZE OF FRESH LEMON JUICE

✤ Prepare a hot grill.

✤ Place the eggplant rounds on a rimmed baking sheet and drizzle with the olive oil, turning to coat both sides. Sprinkle with the salt and let sit for 5 minutes.

✤ Place the rounds on the hot grill and grill until fully cooked, turning halfway through, about 10 minutes total. The rounds will have dark grill lines.

✤ Transfer the eggplant rounds to a platter and sprinkle with the parsley, capers, and garlic. Add the vinegar and lemon juice, toss to coat, and serve.

THE VEG

GRILLED ZUCCHINI WITH ONIONS, CORN, AND CHERRY TOMATOES

When it's summer, especially in August, when the zucchini, corn, and tomatoes are at their peak, we love to fire up the grill for this salad any chance we get. This is a great recipe for entertaining because you can make it ahead, which means you have more time to hang out with your guests.

Serves 6

3 ZUCCHINI, HALVED LENGTHWISE

I LARGE ONION, CUT INTO ½-INCH-THICK RINGS

2 EARS OF FRESH CORN, SHUCKED

3 TABLESPOONS OLIVE OIL

2 TEASPOONS SALT

I PINT CHERRY TOMATOES, HALVED

¼ CUP CHOPPED FRESH PARSLEY

I GARLIC CLOVE, MINCED

I LEMON

FRESHLY GROUND BLACK PEPPER

✤ Prepare a hot grill.

✤ Place the zucchini, onions, and corn on a rimmed baking sheet. Drizzle with 2 tablespoons of the oil and sprinkle with 1 teaspoon of the salt. Toss the vegetables to ensure that they are well coated.

✤ Place the vegetables on the hot grill. As they begin to brown, turn them carefully so that they brown fully on all sides but stay intact, about 3 minutes per side. Remove the vegetables from the grill and let cool slightly.

✤ Cut the grilled corn kernels from the cobs and place in a bowl. Add the cherry tomatoes, the remaining 1 tablespoon olive oil and 1 teaspoon salt, the parsley, and garlic. Squeeze the lemon into the bowl and stir to combine.

✤ Arrange the grilled zucchini on a serving platter. Cut the onion rings in half and drape them over the zucchini. Spoon the tomato and corn mixture over the zucchini and onions. Finish with a grind of pepper and serve warm. Alternatively, make the dish ahead and serve at room temperature.

THE VEG

GRILLING TIPS

We like to cut our veggies on the larger side for grilling so they don't burn quickly. We turn them a few times to keep the insides tender while the outside takes on that ideal smoky char. It's important to remember that your meat and veggies continue to cook after you've pulled them off the grill, so be sure to let the meat rest for 5 minutes before serving and take care to remove the vegetables before they overcook.

CHAPTER

5

THE SALADS

"BY NOW YOU KNOW OUR MANTRA:
MAKE IT, EXPERIENCE IT, SHARE IT."

SIMPLE ARUGULA AND APPLE SALAD

This is far and away the most popular salad at the Shop, where we serve a handful to accompany every sandwich. We prefer Fuji apples because they are crisp and acidic and balance the peppery arugula and sweet apple cider dressing. In most of the restaurants we've worked in, chives are used as a garnish and rarely as an ingredient, but their mild, oniony flavor is absolutely key in this salad. In a pinch, scallions can be used in place of the chives.

Serves 6

ONE 5-OUNCE BAG PREWASHED BABY ARUGULA

I FUJI APPLE, CORED, QUARTERED, SEEDED,
AND THINLY SLICED

¼ CUP THINLY SLICED CHIVES

¼ CUP APPLE CIDER VINAIGRETTE
(RECIPE FOLLOWS)

✤ Combine the arugula, apple, and chives in a large mixing bowl. Dress with the vinaigrette, making sure to lightly toss the greens but thoroughly incorporate the dressing.

QUICK TIP

The Dijon mustard does more than add a vibrant note to the vinaigrette. It provides a stable base that helps the oil and vinegar emulsify, creating that smooth, creamy texture that you want in a vinaigrette. A well-emulsified vinaigrette also evenly coats the lettuce leaves for a balanced salad. Try adding a teaspoon to your basic vinegar-and-olive-oil dressing for a smoother result.

APPLE CIDER VINAIGRETTE

In addition to using this as a dressing for salads, try it as a marinade for grilled meat. This vinaigrette will keep in the fridge for up to three weeks.

Makes 1½ cups

¾ CUP APPLE CIDER

⅓ CUP APPLE CIDER VINEGAR

I TABLESPOON DIJON MUSTARD

½ TEASPOON SALT

I CUP OLIVE OIL

Bring the apple cider to a boil in a small pot over medium-high heat. Reduce the heat to low and simmer until the liquid reduces by half, about 12 minutes.

Pour the cider into a small mixing bowl. Add the vinegar, mustard, and salt and whisk vigorously. While continuing to whisk, slowly drizzle the olive oil into the bowl until completely incorporated.

ROMAINE AND CELERY WITH
SALSA VERDE DRESSING

This is a great, lighter alternative to a Caesar salad—it hits all the same taste notes without the heavy creamy dressing. Don't be afraid of the anchovies in the Salsa Verde. The strong flavor melts away and you're left with a subtle complexity. If you don't say anything, no one will ever know that they're in there. Celery is another of those often-underappreciated vegetables that is worth highlighting, and this salad does just that.

Serves 6

2 HEADS ROMAINE LETTUCE, TOUGH OUTER
LEAVES DISCARDED AND THE REST TORN INTO
BITE-SIZE PIECES

½ BUNCH CELERY, THINLY SLICED,
LEAVES INCLUDED

I CUP GARLIC CROUTONS (PAGE 119)

¼ CUP SALSA VERDE (RECIPE FOLLOWS)

✢ Combine the romaine, celery, and croutons in a large mixing bowl. Dress with the salsa verde, making sure to lightly toss the greens but thoroughly incorporate the dressing.

⌐SALSA VERDE¬

This Italian sauce is traditionally served over fish, but it works really well as a dressing for salads as well as for grilled and roasted meats. Take care not to overprocess it; you definitely want some texture.

Makes 1 cup

¼ CUP SALTED CAPERS, SOAKED IN WARM WATER
FOR 10 MINUTES AND DRAINED

I CUP FRESH PARSLEY LEAVES

¾ CUP OLIVE OIL

JUICE FROM I LEMON

¼ TEASPOON CRUSHED RED PEPPER FLAKES

2 ANCHOVY FILLETS PACKED IN OIL

2 TEASPOONS SALT

Combine the capers, parsley, olive oil, lemon juice, red pepper flakes, anchovies, and salt in a blender. Blend on low speed just until well chopped but still somewhat coarse.

GRILLED MINI CHICKEN BALL SALAD WITH OVEN-DRIED TOMATOES

Grilling gives these balls a nice smoky flavor, but if you're short on time or energy, you can also just warm them in the oven or microwave them, if you prefer. The salad comes together quickly if you use canned beans, and you should always have a stash of our apple cider vinaigrette in the fridge (it can keep for three weeks).

Serves 6

18 COOKED MINI CHICKEN MEATBALLS (PAGE 12), PREPARED AS ¾-INCH MEATBALLS, ROASTED AT 450°F FOR 15 TO 20 MINUTES

2 BUNCHES WATERCRESS, ENDS TRIMMED AND DISCARDED, THE REST CUT INTO 2-INCH-LONG PIECES

1 CUP OVEN-DRIED CHERRY TOMATOES (RECIPE FOLLOWS), AT ROOM TEMPERATURE

2 CUPS WHITE BEANS (PAGE 85) OR RINSED CANNED WHITE BEANS

½ RED ONION, HALVED AND CUT INTO ½-INCH-THICK SLICES

¼ CUP APPLE CIDER VINAIGRETTE (PAGE 112)

✤ Prepare a hot grill. Soak wooden skewers for 5 minutes to prevent them from burning.

✤ Skewer each ball in the center using 3 balls per skewer. Place the skewers on the hot grill and cook, turning them so that the balls are hot and charred on all sides, for about 5 minutes total.

✤ Meanwhile, combine the watercress, cherry tomatoes, beans, and onions in a large bowl. Dress with the apple cider vinaigrette, making sure to lightly toss the salad mixture but thoroughly incorporate the dressing.

✤ Transfer the salad to a large platter or individual bowls and top with the hot chicken balls.

⤙ OVEN-DRIED CHERRY TOMATOES ⤚

While these tomatoes are especially delicious in this salad, make a double batch so you can toss them with roasted veggies, steamed green beans, or sautéed spinach, or spread them as a condiment on your next sandwich. These can be made ahead and kept tightly covered in the fridge for up to one week.

Makes 1 cup

2 PINTS CHERRY TOMATOES, HALVED
6 FRESH THYME SPRIGS
4 GARLIC CLOVES, CRUSHED
2 TEASPOONS SALT
¼ CUP OLIVE OIL

Preheat the oven to 275°F.

Combine the cherry tomatoes, thyme, garlic, salt, and olive oil in a large mixing bowl and toss to thoroughly coat the tomatoes.

Spread out the tomatoes on a large rimmed baking sheet. Bake until the tomatoes are shriveled and sweet but not browned, about 1½ hours. Rotate the pan every 30 minutes for even cooking.

REACH FOR THE RIGHT OIL

Olive oil is an integral part of our cooking. It imparts flavor and is really a workhorse tool in the kitchen. It can be overwhelming to figure out which oil to use but the thing to remember is that the most expensive isn't always the way to go, or necessarily the best tasting. Oftentimes the price is set by the producer so you aren't always paying for quality. Second, many of the costliest oils are created as finishing oils, meaning these concentrated, deeply flavored oils are meant to be drizzled over cooked meat, fish, vegetables, pastas, or soups right before serving. When used this way, their spiced or often bitter flavor adds a layer of complexity that completes the dish. However, when these oils are used for cooking, their flavors can be destroyed by high temperatures or clash with acidic ingredients in a salad dressing.

At the Shop we use a neutral inexpensive extra-virgin olive oil for salad dressings. To finish dishes, we use a strong, spicy, and richly flavored extra-virgin olive oil that gives a kick to whatever we're serving. We use only a drizzle at a time and buy small bottles so the high-quality oil stays fresh. Try buying oils from Spain and Italy, which are easily available, rich in flavor, and reasonably priced.

Olive oil is a sensitive ingredient that can turn rancid if stored improperly. Keep it in a cool, dark place, and buy only as much as you use within a month or two. Don't store olive oil in the cabinet above or next to the stove, as the heat tends to turn the oil rancid more quickly. If your oil has been open for a while, smell it before using. You'll know it's rancid if it has a stale, dusty odor that is reminiscent of mildew or an old attic. If it smells like your grandma's couch, then chuck it. It's not worth ruining a great salad or meal.

AVOCADO AND GRAPEFRUIT SALAD

This salad is all about contrasts. The grapefruit adds a slightly tart punch to the creamy avocado, and the herbs add flavor and texture. This salad comes together in a flash because there's no separate dressing—just a squeeze of lemon and a splash of olive oil.

Serves 4 to 6

1 HEAD BUTTER LETTUCE

2 TABLESPOONS FRESH TARRAGON

2 TABLESPOONS FRESH PARSLEY

2 TABLESPOONS FRESH MINT

2 TABLESPOONS FRESH BASIL

1 SCALLION, THINLY SLICED

¼ CUP OLIVE OIL

JUICE FROM 1 LEMON

SALT TO TASTE

1 LARGE RIPE HAAS AVOCADO, HALVED, PEELED, PITTED, AND CUT INTO ½-INCH DICE

1 LARGE SWEET GRAPEFRUIT, PEELED, AND SLICED INTO ½-INCH ROUNDS, THEN QUARTERED INTO 1-INCH PIECES

FRESHLY GROUND BLACK PEPPER

✤ Combine the lettuce, tarragon, parsley, mint, basil, and scallions in a large mixing bowl. Gently toss with the olive oil, lemon juice, and salt to taste. Fold in the diced avocado and grapefruit gently so as not to break up the avocado.

✤ Divide the salad evenly among salad bowls and finish with a generous grind of pepper.

GRILLED CORN SALAD

To us, corn and ripe tomatoes are the very definition of summer. We never cook corn or serve tomatoes in their off-season, so when summer rolls around, we get really excited and include them in nearly every meal. Don't be afraid to burn the corn and scallions a little here. The charred flavor mixes well with the lime juice and will help to balance the extreme sweetness of the ripe corn.

Serves 6

3 EARS OF FRESH CORN, SHUCKED

I BUNCH SCALLIONS, TRIMMED

3 TABLESPOONS VEGETABLE OIL

2 TEASPOONS SALT

3 LARGE RIPE TOMATOES, CUT INTO LARGE
BITE-SIZE PIECES

6 RADISHES, THINLY SLICED

JUICE FROM I LIME

✤ Prepare a hot grill.

✤ Toss the corn and scallions with 1 tablespoon of the vegetable oil and 1 teaspoon of the salt.

✤ Place the corn and scallions on the hot grill. Turn the corn as it browns so that it is well browned all around. The scallions should be slightly charred in places. Remove the corn and scallions from the grill and let cool slightly.

✤ Cut the grilled corn kernels from the cobs into a medium mixing bowl. Chop the scallions and add them to the bowl. Add the tomatoes, radishes, lime juice, and the remaining 2 tablespoons vegetable oil and 1 teaspoon salt and toss until well incorporated.

ROMAINE, CUCUMBER, AND TOMATO SALAD

This is a refreshing salad that gets a kick from garlic croutons and a creamy tang from the yogurt vinaigrette. It's a simple Mediterranean classic that you will find served all along the coast from North Africa to Spain in the summer months, and is a great companion to The Greek balls (page 10).

Serves 6

I HEAD ROMAINE LETTUCE, TOUGH OUTER
LEAVES DISCARDED AND THE REST TORN INTO
BITE-SIZE PIECES

I CUCUMBER, HALVED LENGTHWISE, QUARTERED,
AND CUT INTO ½-INCH PIECES

I LARGE RIPE TOMATO, CUT INTO ½-INCH PIECES

I CUP GARLIC CROUTONS (RECIPE FOLLOWS)

½ CUP YOGURT VINAIGRETTE (RECIPE FOLLOWS)

✤ Combine the romaine, cucumber, tomatoes, and croutons in a large mixing bowl. Dress with the vinaigrette, making sure to lightly toss the greens but thoroughly incorporate the dressing.

GARLIC CROUTONS

Makes 6 cups

I LARGE LOAF STALE COUNTRY BREAD, CRUSTS REMOVED
I GARLIC CLOVE, MINCED
I CUP FRESH OREGANO, FINELY CHOPPED
¼ CUP OLIVE OIL
SALT

Preheat the oven to 375°F.

Tear the bread into bite-size pieces and place in a large bowl. Add the garlic and oregano and drizzle with the olive oil. Toss gently to combine and season with salt.

Place the croutons on a large rimmed baking sheet and bake for 20 minutes. Stir and continue to bake until the croutons are golden brown and crunchy, checking and stirring every 5 minutes.

YOGURT VINAIGRETTE

Makes 3 cups

2 CUPS BEST-QUALITY PLAIN WHOLE-MILK YOGURT
(NOT GREEK STYLE)
½ RED ONION, FINELY CHOPPED
¼ CUP RED WINE VINEGAR
½ CUP OLIVE OIL
2 TEASPOONS SALT

Combine the yogurt, onions, vinegar, olive oil, and salt in a large mixing bowl. Whisk until smooth and thoroughly combined.

PERSIMMON SALAD

This jewel of a salad is the prettiest way to welcome in the cooler months. We use the firm fuyu persimmons, which have a crunch similar to that of apples. The pomegranate seeds add a gorgeous touch and a resounding sweet and tart pop of flavor.

Serves 6

2 BELGIAN ENDIVES, CORED, CUT INTO
1-INCH SLICES

1 HEAD RADICCHIO, CORED, LEAVES CUT INTO
3-INCH PIECES

ONE 5-OUNCE BAG BABY ARUGULA

1 HEAD FRISÉE, CORE AND DARK GREEN LEAVES
DISCARDED, WHITE LEAVES CUT INTO
2-INCH PIECES

2 FUYU PERSIMMONS, PEELED, CORED, HALVED,
AND SLICED INTO THIN WEDGES

¼ CUP WALNUTS, TOASTED AND FINELY CHOPPED

1 POMEGRANATE, SEEDS REMOVED AND
RESERVED, PITH AND SKIN DISCARDED

¼ CUP POMEGRANATE VINAIGRETTE
(RECIPE FOLLOWS)

FRESHLY GROUND BLACK PEPPER

✤ Combine the endive, radicchio, arugula, frisée, persimmons, walnuts, and one-quarter of the pomegranate seeds (reserve the rest for the vinaigrette) in a large mixing bowl. Dress with the vinaigrette, making sure to lightly toss the greens but thoroughly incorporate the dressing. Finish with a generous grind of the pepper mill.

⁓ POMEGRANATE VINAIGRETTE ⁓

This vinaigrette is fabulous spooned over roasted veggies and grilled eggplant.

Makes 2 cups

½ CUP POMEGRANATE SEEDS
½ CUP SHERRY VINEGAR
½ CUP HONEY
1 TABLESPOON DIJON MUSTARD
1 TEASPOON SALT
1¼ CUPS OLIVE OIL

Combine the pomegranate seeds, vinegar, honey, mustard, and salt in a blender. Process on high speed until the seeds have been pulverized and have released all of their juices. Reduce the speed to low, carefully remove the lid, and slowly drizzle in the olive oil to incorporate.

Strain through a fine-mesh strainer and serve.

QUICK TIP

You can often buy pomegranate seeds that already have been removed from the fruit. However, whole pomegranates are great to have. They keep well in the fruit bin and can be cut in half and juiced and added to your OJ. For this recipe, cut the pomegranate into quarters. Gently peel the seeds away from the skin, being careful because the juices will definitely stain your cutting board and clothing.

KABOCHA SQUASH SALAD

Kabocha is a Japanese winter squash or pumpkin that has a slight sweetness that we accentuate by simmering it with sugar. You can substitute peeled butternut squash if your market doesn't carry kabocha, but look for it. These days it's often in bins at the bottom of supermarket produce aisles.

Serves 6

I CUP SUGAR

I TABLESPOON PLUS A PINCH OF SALT

¼ UNPEELED KABOCHA SQUASH, SEEDED AND CUT INTO ½-INCH CUBES (ABOUT 1½ CUPS)

I HEAD ROMAINE LETTUCE, TORN INTO BITE-SIZE PIECES

4 OUNCES BABY ARUGULA, WASHED AND PATTED DRY

¼ CUP ROASTED, SHELLED PUMPKIN SEEDS

I TEASPOON OLIVE OIL

6 SCALLIONS, THINLY SLICED

¼ CUP SHERRY VINAIGRETTE (RECIPE FOLLOWS)

✦ Fill a medium saucepan with 3 cups water and bring to a boil. Stir in the sugar and salt to dissolve. Add the squash and cook until tender but not falling apart, about 5 minutes. Strain the squash and place in the refrigerator to cool completely.

✦ Combine the squash, romaine, arugula, pumpkin seeds, olive oil, and scallions in a large mixing bowl. Dress with the vinaigrette and toss gently so as not to break up the squash.

SHERRY VINAIGRETTE

Sherry vinegar is another gift to the pantry from Spain that we keep alongside our saffron and olive oils.

Makes 2 cups

½ CUP SHERRY VINEGAR

I TABLESPOON DIJON MUSTARD

I TEASPOON SALT

I CUP OLIVE OIL

Combine the vinegar, mustard, and salt in a blender. Blend on low speed while slowly drizzling in the olive oil.

EVERYTHING BUT
THE KITCHEN SINK SALAD

This salad is a permanent feature on our menu. It starts with simple greens, then is topped with a selection of market vegetables, three balls, and the sauce of your choice. When topped with veggie balls, it's a serious vegetarian meal, but you can also top it with any ball you'd like (heat up your balls in the microwave for a minute or two to take the chill off). Ladle on your favorite warm sauce in place of the expected dressing.

Serves 4 to 6

1 TABLESPOON OLIVE OIL

1 LARGE PORTABELLO MUSHROOM, STEM
DISCARDED, CAP CUT INTO 1-INCH PIECES

PINCH OF SALT

½ BUNCH ASPARAGUS, TRIMMED AND CUT INTO
2-INCH PIECES

1 HEAD ROMAINE LETTUCE, TOUGH OUTER LEAVES
DISCARDED AND THE REST TORN INTO
BITE-SIZE PIECES

½ FENNEL HEAD, THINLY SLICED

¼ CUP SHERRY VINAIGRETTE (PAGE 121)

12 WARM VEGGIE BALLS (PAGE 16) OR
MEATBALLS OF YOUR CHOOSING

✤ Heat the olive oil in a large saucepan over medium heat. Add the mushrooms and salt and sauté until they begin to brown and their liquid has evaporated, about 10 minutes. Transfer to a bowl and let cool in the refrigerator.

✤ Bring a medium pot half full of generously salted water to a boil. Add the asparagus and cook for 2½ minutes. Strain and cool the asparagus under cold running water.

✤ Combine the mushrooms, asparagus, romaine, fennel, and vinaigrette in a large mixing bowl and toss to coat. Transfer to a serving platter and top with warm balls.

THE SALADS

LENTIL AND BUTTER LETTUCE
SALAD

French green lentils, or *lentilles du Puy,* are smaller and more delicate in flavor than the usual supermarket variety. They require only fifteen minutes of cooking too, which makes them a handy pantry staple. A drizzle of crème fraîche and heavy cream sends this dish over the top.

Serves 6

½ CUP FRENCH GREEN LENTILS

I TEASPOON GROUND CUMIN

I HEAD BUTTER LETTUCE, TORN INTO BITE-SIZE PIECES

½ CUP FRESH CILANTRO, PLUS MORE FOR GARNISH

6 SCALLIONS, THINLY SLICED

¼ CUP SHERRY VINAIGRETTE (PAGE 121)

¼ CUP CRÈME FRAÎCHE OR SOUR CREAM

I TABLESPOON HEAVY CREAM

✤ Bring 3 cups salted water to a boil in a small pot. Add the lentils and cook until just tender, about 15 minutes. Drain and allow to cool.

✤ Combine the cool lentils with the cumin in a large mixing bowl. Add the lettuce, cilantro, scallions, and vinaigrette. Gently toss to combine so as not to bruise the lettuce.

✤ Combine the crème fraîche and cream in a small bowl.

✤ Divide the salad evenly among serving bowls and drizzle with the crème fraîche mixture. Sprinkle with additional cilantro, if desired.

CHAPTER

6

THE
SWEETS

"WE OFFER ONLY ONE DESSERT, BECAUSE C'MON,
IS THERE REALLY ANYTHING BETTER THAN AN
ICE-CREAM SANDWICH?"

GINGER COOKIES

These cookies pack a triple punch with ground ginger, freshly grated ginger, and crystallized ginger. A touch of honey tempers the bite and adds richness. We love to build these into sandwiches with Cinnamon Ice Cream (page 143) in the winter or Plum Sorbet (page 144) in the summer.

Makes about 2 dozen 3-inch cookies

12 TABLESPOONS (1½ STICKS) UNSALTED BUTTER

1 CUP SUGAR

1 LARGE EGG

2 CUPS ALL-PURPOSE FLOUR

1½ TEASPOONS BAKING SODA

¼ TEASPOON SALT

1 TABLESPOON GROUND GINGER

1 TABLESPOON GRATED FRESH GINGER

¼ CUP CRYSTALLIZED GINGER, FINELY DICED

2 TABLESPOONS HONEY

✤ Preheat the oven to 350°F. Butter two 12 × 17-inch rimmed baking sheets. Set aside.

✤ Cream the butter and sugar together in a large mixing bowl with a hand mixer on high speed until light and fluffy, about 3 minutes. Add the egg and continue to mix on low speed until just incorporated.

✤ Mix together the flour, baking soda, salt, and ground ginger in a bowl. Add half of the flour mixture to the butter mixture and mix to combine. Add the fresh ginger, crystallized ginger, and honey and mix to combine. Add the remaining flour mixture and mix to combine. The dough should be fairly sticky.

✤ Chill the dough in a bowl covered with plastic wrap in the refrigerator for at least 30 minutes.

✤ Using a small ice-cream scooper, scoop the dough into 1-inch balls and place on the prepared baking sheets, leaving at least 2 inches between cookies.

✤ Bake for 12 minutes, rotating the pan halfway through baking, until the cookies are brown around the edges and lightly colored in the center.

✤ Let the cookies cool on the baking sheet for 2 minutes before transferring them with a spatula to a wire cooling rack to fully cool.

PEANUT BUTTER–CHOCOLATE
ICEBOX COOKIES

No baking required, so these are a fast and easy sugar fix! Just make sure the baking sheets fit in your fridge; otherwise, make some room and lay the sheets of waxed paper directly on the fridge shelf. These are also great to make with kids because there's no hot stuff to fear. We like to layer these with Vanilla or Chocolate Ice Cream (pages 136 and 137), but Caramel (page 139) is pretty awesome too. The cookies will keep in the refrigerator for 1 week.

Makes about thirty 2½-inch cookies

12 TABLESPOONS (1½ STICKS) UNSALTED BUTTER,
AT ROOM TEMPERATURE

1 CUP CREAMY PEANUT BUTTER

1½ CUPS CONFECTIONERS' SUGAR

ONE 13.5-OUNCE BOX GRAHAM CRACKER CRUMBS

ONE 12-OUNCE BAG SEMISWEET
CHOCOLATE CHIPS

✤ Using a stand mixer, cream the butter, peanut butter, and ½ cup of the confectioners' sugar until light and fluffy, about 3 minutes. Stir in the graham cracker crumbs and mix until a stiff, crumbly dough forms.

✤ Lay out two 24-inch lengths of waxed paper, overlapping them to produce a large square.

✤ Dust the waxed paper with ½ cup of the remaining confectioners' sugar. Dump the dough onto the prepared surface, patting the dough together into a large, flat sheet. Dust with the remaining ½ cup confectioners' sugar and roll out with a rolling pin to slightly less than ¼ inch thick.

✤ Melt the chocolate chips in the top of a double boiler over medium heat. Spread the melted chocolate over the sheet of cookie dough with a flat metal spatula until evenly coated. Transfer the dough to the refrigerator for 10 minutes. The chocolate should cool and become semi-hardened.

✤ Remove the dough from the refrigerator and cut out cookies with a 2½-inch round cutter. Place the cookies on three waxed paper–lined 12 × 17-inch baking sheets and refrigerate until ready to serve, at least 2 hours. The cookies must be completely chilled before serving.

COCONUT MACAROONS

When you think of a macaroon, you think of a high, rounded cookie. Think again. At the Shop we flatten them to accommodate ice cream in the middle. We love the toasted coconut flavor of the cookies, or for a nostalgic twist, try almond extract instead of the vanilla. Paired with Chocolate Ice Cream (page 137), it's practically an Almond Joy!

Makes 2 dozen 2½-inch cookies

ONE 14-OUNCE BAG SWEETENED SHREDDED
COCONUT

⅓ CUP SUGAR

3 LARGE EGG WHITES

1 TABLESPOON PURE VANILLA EXTRACT

3 TABLESPOONS SWEETENED CONDENSED MILK

❖ Preheat the oven to 300°F. Butter two 12 x 17-inch rimmed baking sheets. Set aside.

❖ Combine the coconut, sugar, egg whites, vanilla, and condensed milk in a large bowl and mix to incorporate.

❖ Using a small ice-cream scooper, scoop the dough into 1-inch balls and place on the prepared baking sheets, leaving 3 inches between cookies. Flatten each cookie with the palm of your hand to create 2½-inch cookies.

❖ Bake for about 40 minutes, rotating the pan halfway through baking, until the edges of the cookies are a golden brown.

❖ Let the cookies cool on the baking sheets for 2 minutes before transferring them with a spatula to wire cooling racks to fully cool.

BROWNIE COOKIES

Paired with Espresso Ice Cream (page 140), this is even better than a brownie sundae! Use the best-quality bittersweet chocolate chips you can find for a richer flavor. We like the way the white chocolate chips give a graphic pop to the cookie. For a superintense chocoholic experience, add a scoop of Chocolate Ice Cream (page 137).

Makes about 3 dozen 3-inch cookies

3 CUPS BITTERSWEET CHOCOLATE CHIPS

11 TABLESPOONS UNSALTED BUTTER

6 LARGE EGGS

1 CUP FIRMLY PACKED DARK BROWN SUGAR

1 CUP GRANULATED SUGAR

1 TABLESPOON PURE VANILLA EXTRACT

2 CUPS ALL-PURPOSE FLOUR

1 TEASPOON BAKING POWDER

½ TEASPOON SALT

2 CUPS SEMISWEET CHOCOLATE CHIPS

2 CUPS WHITE CHOCOLATE CHIPS

1 CUP WALNUTS, ROUGHLY CHOPPED

✦ Melt the bittersweet chocolate chips and the butter in the top of a double boiler over medium heat. Set aside to cool to room temperature.

✦ Beat the eggs, brown sugar, granulated sugar, and vanilla in a large bowl with a whisk until combined. Add the melted chocolate and butter and whisk to incorporate.

✦ Mix together the flour, baking powder, and salt in a bowl. Add the flour mixture to the chocolate mixture in two batches, stirring after each addition until fully incorporated. Add the semisweet chocolate chips, white chocolate chips, and walnuts and stir to combine.

✦ Chill the dough in the refrigerator for at least 1 hour.

✦ Preheat the oven to 350°F. Butter three 12 × 17–inch rimmed baking sheets. Set aside.

✦ Using an ice-cream scooper, scoop the dough into 1-inch balls and place on the prepared baking sheets, leaving at least 2 inches between cookies.

✦ Bake for 14 minutes, rotating the pan halfway through baking, until the edges of the cookies are slightly darker but the centers are soft.

✦ Let the cookies cool on the baking sheets for 2 minutes before transferring them with a spatula to wire cooling racks to fully cool.

CHOCOLATE CHIP COOKIES

There's a reason chocolate chip cookies are the classic American favorite. We bet some of these never even meet a cooling rack, let alone a cookie jar. We like 'em semisoft and paired with vanilla ice cream—the most popular combo at the Shop by far. Try them with our fresh Mint Ice Cream (page 142) for a refreshing sandwich twist.

Makes 3 dozen 3-inch cookies

8 TABLESPOONS (I STICK) UNSALTED BUTTER

⅓ CUP FIRMLY PACKED DARK BROWN SUGAR

I CUP GRANULATED SUGAR

I LARGE EGG

I LARGE EGG WHITE

2 TEASPOONS PURE VANILLA EXTRACT

2 CUPS ALL-PURPOSE FLOUR

I TEASPOON BAKING SODA

I TEASPOON SALT

2½ CUPS SEMISWEET CHOCOLATE CHIPS, FINELY CHOPPED

✤ Cream the butter, brown sugar, and granulated sugar in a large mixing bowl with a hand mixer on high speed until light and fluffy, about 3 minutes. Add the egg, egg white, and vanilla and continue to mix on low speed until just incorporated.

✤ Mix together the flour, baking soda, and salt in a bowl. Add the flour mixture to the butter mixture on low speed, mixing slowly until just combined (do not overmix). Fold in the chocolate chips using a wooden spoon or stiff spatula.

✤ Chill the dough covered in plastic wrap in the refrigerator for 30 minutes.

✤ Preheat the oven to 350°F. Butter three 12 × 17-inch rimmed baking sheets. Set aside.

✤ Using an ice-cream scooper, scoop the dough into 1-inch balls and place on the prepared baking sheets, leaving at least 2 inches between cookies.

✤ Bake for 12 minutes, rotating the pans halfway through baking, until the edges of the cookies are golden brown but the centers are soft.

✤ Let the cookies cool on the baking sheets for 2 minutes before transferring them with a spatula to wire cooling racks to fully cool.

OATMEAL-APPLE-RAISIN COOKIES

Complete comfort food . . . Layer these with our Cinnamon Ice Cream (page 143) and savor the spicy-sweet goodness of this sandwich. Try using freshly grated nutmeg instead of ground—you'll be surprised by the difference.

Makes about thirty 3-inch cookies

THE SWEETS

12 TABLESPOONS (1½ STICKS) UNSALTED BUTTER

1½ CUPS FIRMLY PACKED DARK BROWN SUGAR

½ CUP APPLE BUTTER

1 LARGE EGG

1 CUP ALL-PURPOSE FLOUR

½ TEASPOON BAKING SODA

½ TEASPOON GROUND CINNAMON

½ TEASPOON GROUND CLOVES

¼ TEASPOON GROUND NUTMEG

¼ TEASPOON SALT

½ CUP DARK RAISINS

1 APPLE, PEELED, CORED, SEEDED, AND FINELY DICED

4 CUPS OLD-FASHIONED ROLLED OATS

✤ Preheat the oven to 350°F. Butter three 12 × 17-inch rimmed baking sheets. Set aside.

✤ Cream the butter and brown sugar together in a large mixing bowl with a hand mixer on high speed until light and fluffy, about 3 minutes. Add the apple butter and mix until well blended. Add the egg and mix on low speed until just incorporated.

✤ Mix together the flour, baking soda, cinnamon, cloves, nutmeg, and salt in a bowl. Add the flour mixture to the butter mixture on low speed and combine. Add the raisins, apples, and oats and gently mix to incorporate.

✤ Using a small ice-cream scooper, scoop the dough into 1-inch balls. Place on the prepared baking sheets, leaving at least 2 inches between cookies. Flatten each cookie slightly with the palm of your hand.

✤ Bake for 15 minutes, rotating the pan halfway through baking, until the edges of the cookies are light brown.

✤ Let the cookies cool on the baking sheets for 2 minutes before transferring them with a spatula to wire cooling racks to fully cool.

CHOCOLATE WALNUT
MERINGUES

This is a sophisticated but really simple cookie that can be used as a base for a range of add-ins. Once you've gotten your egg whites nice and glossy, try adding dried cherries or substitute almonds or pistachios for the walnuts. Orange zest and chocolate is another good combination. Which ice cream to consider? Besides the obvious Chocolate Ice Cream (page 137), Espresso Ice Cream (page 140) is another winner.

Makes 2 dozen 3-inch cookies

¾ CUP EGG WHITES (FROM 7 OR 8 LARGE EGGS)

½ TEASPOON SALT

¼ TEASPOON CREAM OF TARTAR

I CUP SUGAR

I TABLESPOON PURE VANILLA EXTRACT

1¾ CUPS CHOPPED SEMISWEET CHOCOLATE

2 CUPS FINELY CHOPPED WALNUTS

✤ Preheat the oven to 275°F. Line two 12 × 17-inch rimmed baking sheets with parchment paper.

✤ Using a stand mixer, whip the egg whites for 4 minutes until foamy. Add the salt and cream of tartar. Add the sugar gradually and continue whipping for about 2 more minutes until the egg whites reach a stiff peak and are glossy. Whisk in the vanilla. Fold in the chocolate and walnuts.

✤ Drop the meringue mixture by rounded tablespoonfuls onto the prepared baking sheets and gently flatten and shape into a circle.

✤ Bake for 50 minutes, rotating the pans halfway through baking, until the centers of the meringues are firm to the touch.

✤ Let the meringues cool on the baking sheets for 2 minutes before transferring them with a spatula to a wire cooling rack to fully cool.

QUICK TIP

This cookie is a great surprise and change from the usual butter and sugar cookies used for sandies. It's simple to make, but its success depends on properly whipped egg whites. The key is to gradually add the sugar so the egg whites build their structure and become firm and quite glossy. In fact, you should be able to hold the bowl with the fully whipped whites upside down over your head without the whites falling out, though we really don't recommend this in practice! Be sure to fold in the chocolate and the walnuts gently so you don't deflate all the air that you've incorporated.

VANILLA ICE CREAM

This basic recipe calls for only six ingredients, but the result is rich and creamy and utterly satisfying. Pair it with any of the cookies in this chapter for a righteous ice-cream sandwich or enjoy it simply on its own.

Makes 2 quarts

3 CUPS HEAVY CREAM

1 TEASPOON PURE VANILLA EXTRACT

2½ CUPS WHOLE MILK

1⅓ CUPS SUGAR

2 VANILLA BEANS, SPLIT IN HALF LENGTHWISE
AND SEEDS SCRAPED FROM THE PODS

7 LARGE EGG YOLKS

✤ Combine the cream and vanilla extract in a large pot. Set a large strainer over the pot and set aside.

✤ Bring the milk, half of the sugar, and the vanilla beans to a boil in a medium pot over medium heat, stirring frequently. Once at a boil, reduce heat to low.

✤ Whisk the egg yolks with the remaining sugar in a large bowl. Temper the yolks by slowly drizzling 1 cup of the hot milk mixture into the bowl while whisking vigorously. Slowly pour the tempered egg mixture into the pot of hot milk and continue to cook, whisking constantly, until the mixture begins to thicken, coats the back of a metal spoon, and reaches 170°F on an instant-read thermometer (note that the mixture can easily overcook and curdle, so be sure not to bring the mixture to a boil). Strain the mixture into the pot with the reserved cream and vanilla and stir to incorporate.

✤ Refrigerate until fully cool before following your ice-cream maker's manufacturer's suggestions for freezing.

CHOCOLATE ICE CREAM

his ice cream combines two different forms of chocolate for a doubly intense chocolate experience.

Makes 2 quarts

1½ CUPS HEAVY CREAM

2 TEASPOONS PURE VANILLA EXTRACT

½ TEASPOON SALT

3½ CUPS WHOLE MILK

1½ CUPS SUGAR

¼ CUP UNSWEETENED COCOA POWDER

2 CUPS BITTERSWEET CHOCOLATE CHIPS

6 LARGE EGG YOLKS

❖ Combine the cream, vanilla, and salt in a large pot. Set a large strainer over the pot and set aside.

❖ Bring the milk, half of the sugar, and the cocoa powder to a boil in a medium pot over medium heat, stirring frequently. Once at a boil, reduce heat to low.

❖ Stir in the chocolate chips, stirring constantly until they are completely melted and incorporated.

❖ Whisk the egg yolks with the remaining sugar in a large bowl. Temper the yolks by slowly drizzling 1 cup of the hot chocolate-milk mixture into the bowl while whisking vigorously. Slowly pour the tempered egg mixture into the pot of hot milk and continue to cook, whisking constantly, until the mixture begins to thicken, coats the back of a metal spoon, and reaches 170°F on an instant-read thermometer (note that the mixture can easily overcook and curdle, so be sure not to bring the mixture to a boil). Strain the mixture into the pot with the reserved cream and vanilla and stir to incorporate.

❖ Refrigerate until fully cool before following your ice-cream maker's manufacturer's suggestions for freezing.

STRAWBERRY ICE CREAM

his is an ideal ice cream for early summer, when strawberries are at their peak of flavor.

Makes 2 quarts

2 PINTS STRAWBERRIES, WASHED AND STEMMED,
PLUS I PINT, WASHED, STEMMED,
AND FINELY DICED

2½ CUPS SUGAR

2 CUPS HEAVY CREAM

I TEASPOON PURE VANILLA EXTRACT

2 CUPS WHOLE MILK

6 LARGE EGG YOLKS

✤ Combine the 2 pints whole strawberries with 1½ cups of the sugar in a food processor and puree. Combine the puree, cream, and vanilla in a large pot. Set a large strainer over the pot and set aside.

✤ Bring the milk and ½ cup of the remaining sugar to a boil in a medium pot over medium heat, stirring frequently. Once at a boil, reduce heat to low.

✤ Whisk the egg yolks with the remaining ½ cup sugar in a large bowl. Temper the yolks by slowly drizzling 1 cup of the hot milk mixture into the bowl while whisking vigorously. Slowly pour the tempered eggs into the pot of hot milk and continue to cook, mixing constantly, until the mixture begins to thicken, coats the back of a metal spoon, and reaches 170°F on an instant-read thermometer (note that the mixture can easily overcook and curdle, so be sure not to bring the mixture to a boil). Strain the mixture into the pot with the reserved puree, cream, and vanilla and stir to incorporate.

✤ Refrigerate until fully cool before following your ice-cream maker's manufacturer's suggestions for freezing. Fold in the remaining diced strawberries before freezing.

THE SWEETS

CARAMEL ICE CREAM

This rich, buttery ice cream is the perfect blend of sweet with a hint of salty. Try it between Peanut Butter–Chocolate Icebox Cookies (page 129) or Brownie Cookies (page 131).

Makes 2 quarts

2¼ CUPS SUGAR

6 TABLESPOONS UNSALTED BUTTER

1 TEASPOON SALT

1½ CUPS HEAVY CREAM

3 CUPS WHOLE MILK

8 LARGE EGG YOLKS

2 TEASPOONS PURE VANILLA EXTRACT

✤ To make the caramel, combine 1½ cups of the sugar with ¼ cup water in a medium-size heavy-bottomed pot over medium heat and cook until the mixture turns a golden amber, about 6 minutes. Remove from the heat and carefully stir in the butter and salt (the mixture will bubble and sputter vigorously). Slowly stir in the cream and milk and return to the heat. Whisk until the mixture is smooth and any bits of caramel have dissolved.

✤ Whisk the egg yolks with the remaining ¾ cup sugar in a large bowl. Temper the yolks by slowly drizzling 1 cup of the hot caramel mixture into the bowl while whisking vigorously. Slowly pour the tempered eggs into the pot of caramel and continue to cook, mixing constantly, until the mixture begins to thicken, coats the back of a metal spoon, and reaches 170°F on an instant-read thermometer (note that the mixture can easily overcook and curdle, so be sure not to bring the mixture to a boil). Strain the mixture into a bowl and stir in the vanilla until fully incorporated.

✤ Refrigerate until fully cool before following your ice-cream maker's manufacturer's suggestions for freezing.

ESPRESSO ICE CREAM

Like an iced latte on steroids, our espresso ice cream is sure to keep you up and running. It's as potent as it is delicious, so we suggest it for an afternoon dessert and not for late-night consumption.

Makes 2 quarts

3½ CUPS HEAVY CREAM

¼ CUP (2 OUNCES) BREWED ESPRESSO

⅓ CUP INSTANT COFFEE GRANULES OR 3 TABLESPOONS INSTANT ESPRESSO POWDER

½ TEASPOON PURE VANILLA EXTRACT

2 CUPS WHOLE MILK

I CUP SUGAR

8 LARGE EGG YOLKS

✤ Combine the cream, espresso, coffee granules, and vanilla in a large pot. Set a large strainer over the pot and set aside.

✤ Bring the milk and ½ cup of the sugar to a boil in a medium pot over medium heat, stirring frequently. Once at a boil, reduce heat to low.

✤ Whisk the egg yolks with the remaining ½ cup sugar in a large bowl. Temper the yolks by slowly drizzling 1 cup of the hot milk mixture into the bowl while whisking vigorously. Slowly pour the tempered eggs into the pot of hot milk mixture and continue to cook, mixing constantly, until the mixture begins to thicken, coats the back of a metal spoon, and reaches 170°F on an instant-read thermometer (note that the mixture can easily overcook and curdle, so be sure not to bring the mixture to a boil). Strain the mixture into the pot with the reserved cream, espresso, coffee, granules, and vanilla and stir to incorporate.

✤ Refrigerate until fully cool before following your ice-cream maker's manufacturer's suggestions for freezing.

MINT ICE CREAM

uests are often surprised by the fresh mint flavor of this ice cream. The trick is adding raw chopped mint after the ice cream is cooled.

Makes 2 quarts

3 CUPS HEAVY CREAM

1½ TEASPOONS PURE VANILLA EXTRACT

1 BUNCH FRESH MINT, PLUS 1 CUP MINT LEAVES, FINELY CHOPPED

2½ CUPS WHOLE MILK

1⅓ CUPS SUGAR

7 LARGE EGG YOLKS

✤ Combine the cream, vanilla, and chopped mint in a large pot and set aside.

✤ Bring the milk, half of the sugar, and the bunch of mint to a boil in a medium pot over medium heat, stirring frequently. Once the mixture is at a boil, remove from the heat and allow to steep for 30 minutes.

✤ Remove the mint from the pot and bring the mixture back up to a boil. Once at a boil, reduce heat to low. Whisk the egg yolks with the remaining sugar in a large bowl. Temper the yolks by slowly drizzling 1 cup of the hot milk mixture into the bowl while whisking vigorously. Slowly pour the tempered eggs into the pot of hot milk and cook over low heat, mixing constantly, until the mixture begins to thicken, coats the back of a metal spoon, and reaches 170°F on an instant-read thermometer (note that the mixture can easily overcook and curdle, so be sure not to bring the mixture to a boil). Strain the mixture into the pot with the reserved cream and vanilla and stir to incorporate.

✤ Refrigerate until fully cool before following your ice-cream maker's manufacturer's suggestions for freezing.

THE SWEETS

CINNAMON ICE CREAM

This ice cream has a custardlike flavor and texture. The taste improves and mellows if the ice cream is left to sit for a day in the freezer.

Makes 2 quarts

6 CUPS WHOLE MILK

1⅓ CUPS SUGAR

2 VANILLA BEANS, SPLIT IN HALF LENGTHWISE
AND SEEDS SCRAPED FROM THE PODS

2 TABLESPOONS GROUND CINNAMON

2 BAY LEAVES

8 LARGE EGG YOLKS

✦ Set a large strainer over a large pot and set aside.

✦ Bring the milk, half of the sugar, the vanilla beans and seeds, the cinnamon, and bay leaves to a boil in a medium pot over medium heat, stirring frequently. Once at a boil, reduce heat to low.

✦ Whisk the egg yolks with the remaining sugar in a large bowl. Temper the yolks by slowly drizzling 1 cup of the hot milk mixture into the bowl while whisking vigorously. Slowly pour the tempered eggs into the pot of hot milk and cook over low heat, mixing constantly, until the mixture begins to thicken, coats the back of a metal spoon, and reaches 170°F on an instant-read thermometer (note that the mixture can easily overcook and curdle so be sure not to bring the mixture to a boil). Strain the mixture into the pot with the strainer, discarding the vanilla beans and bay leaves. Stir to incorporate.

✦ Refrigerate until fully cool before following your ice-cream maker's manufacturer's suggestions for freezing.

PLUM SORBET

little sweet with just the right amount of sour. We love this sorbet sandwiched between Chocolate Walnut Meringues (page 135).

Makes 2 quarts

4 POUNDS RIPE PLUMS, HALVED AND PITTED

2 CUPS FIRMLY PACKED LIGHT BROWN SUGAR

½ CUP GRANULATED SUGAR

⅓ CUP FRESH LEMON JUICE

✤ Bring the plums, brown sugar, and granulated sugar to a boil in a large pot. Cook over medium heat until the plums have broken down, about 5 minutes.

✤ Transfer the plum mixture to a food processor, add the lemon juice, and puree.

✤ Refrigerate until fully cool before following your ice-cream maker's manufacturer's suggestions for freezing.

"MAKE MEATBALLS PART OF YOUR LIFE.
THEY'RE WORTH IT!"

ACKNOWLEDGMENTS

Let's just say that without our moms, there'd be no Meatball Shop. So, first and foremost, we have to give them a big shout-out!

Daniel: My mother is extremely kindhearted, and possesses a pure and beautiful soul. She's an artist and has had an enormous influence on me beyond food, but food is a strong bond in our lives. She inspired me to cook early in my life and has supported me through every job from my early days through my current adventures. When it came time to build The Meatball Shop, my mother stopped by every day after her own job to help with construction, to clean, to paint, and to decorate. We worked late into the night together to design and build the mosaic that marks the restaurant entrance. My mother remains a deeply honest voice that I can always trust. The restaurant would not be what it is without her influence. Thank you.

Michael: My mom has believed in me and indulged and supported all of my decisions—some more than others! When we first opened the restaurant, she not only helped us set up the bookkeeping, but also organized her New Jersey community to make multiple trips to the Shop to help support us. Her guidance and insight helped Dan and me find our way in through the tough transition from being friends to business partners.

And my mom's cooking helped shape the Shop too. While she wasn't a four-star chef, her homey, cozy food nourished my soul and was the comfort that sustained me, and it was that kind of vibe that I wanted to re-create with the restaurant. I get hungry just thinking about her cooking.

I'm lucky to be so tight with my mom. She gave me my greatest character trait, which is my voice, and I learned it all from her. Mom, I love ya!

Now that we've properly thanked our moms, it's on to everyone else . . .

We do have partners behind the scenes who have worked tirelessly to make the Shop a success: Josh Greenstein, Larry Praeger, Eli Holzman, and Doctor Peter Praeger. Thank you guys for sharing our dream with us.

We opened The Meatball Shop with one manager, Mike's friend from culinary school, Scott Jaffe. Without Scotty we simply wouldn't be where we are today; we made Scotty the chef of the Shop shortly after opening. Hiring Scotty was the single best decision we've made. A few weeks after the shop opened, Damien Domenack answered our prayers when he saw our ad on Craigslist for a front-of-house manager. He quickly grew into his current role as the general manager. Damien, you are the glue, grease, gears, and gas keepin' her runnin'. Thank you, man.

Mike's wife, Donna, as our opening pastry chef, worked for months to create recipes for cookies and ice cream; she worked her tail off, and many of her recipes are still on the menu.

Shortly before opening the shop, Phil Baltz took a chance when he took us on as clients at his publicity firm Baltz and Company. Our publicity team of Sarah Abell and Camil Ferenczi are second to none. They put us on the map and keep the seats filled every night. Thanks for being part of the family.

Our dreams would never have been realized in this book without the vision, help, support, and hard work of our agents from WME. Eric Lupfer, Josh Bider, Suzanne Lyon, and Jason Hodes, thank you for believing in us and for making this happen. A big thank-you to the crew at Ballantine Books, especially our editor, Pamela Cannon, who has definitely been the most important person in this process. We owe you one; it's been a blast!

A lot of work goes into writing a book, and we could not have pulled it off without the help of Lauren Deen. Thank you for the long nights and for echoing our voices so well. We've made a couple of friends along the way to publishing this book, including photographer John Kernick and food stylist Allison Attenborough. John is a magician with a camera who never misses a shot and will keep you smiling throughout the entire process. That, coupled with Allison's impeccable taste and style, yielded the beautiful photographs for this book. And a big shout-out to Alison Ladman for her spot-on recipe testing and additions.

In closing, we've had far too much help from far too many people to try to thank you all. We could easily fill an entire chapter and still not mention most of you. Suffice it to say that anybody who has ever worked in the Shop or eaten our food has played a large part in our success. So, thank you!

NOTE: *When more than one page number appears next to a recipe, the* **bold** *number indicates the location of the recipe.*

INDEX

ABOUT THE AUTHORS

DANIEL HOLZMAN is executive chef at The Meatball Shop. He is an alum of Le Bernardin, San Francisco's Fifth Floor, and Aqua, among other highly acclaimed restaurants. He attended the Culinary Institute of America, where he received a full scholarship from The James Beard Foundation.

MICHAEL CHERNOW runs the front-of-house operations and the beverage program at The Meatball Shop. He has worked extensively in restaurants in New York and Los Angeles. He is a graduate of the French Culinary Institute, where he earned degrees in culinary arts and restaurant management. He and Holzman met as teenagers when they worked together as delivery boys at the New York vegan restaurant Candle Cafe. Needless to say, the vegan thing didn't really stick.

LAUREN DEEN is the author of the *New York Times* bestselling *Cook Yourself Thin* series and *Kitchen Playdates*. She is an Emmy award– and James Beard award–winning television producer and director. She is currently executive producer of *food(ography)* on the Cooking Channel.

ABOUT THE TYPE

This book was set in Caslon, a typeface first designed in 1722 by William Caslon. Its widespread use by most English printers in the early eighteenth century soon supplanted the Dutch typefaces that had formerly prevailed. The roman is considered a "workhorse" typeface due to its pleasant, open appearance, while the italic is exceedingly decorative.